AN ANSWER
To
HUMANISTIC
PSYCHOLOGY

Nelson Hinman

HARVEST HOUSE PUBLISHERS
Irvine, California 92714

AN ANSWER TO HUMANISTIC PSYCHOLOGY

Copyright © 1980 by Harvest House Publishers
Irvine, California 92714

(Original edition Copyright © 1979 by Church of The Highlands, San Bruno, California, under the title **Biblical Alternatives to Humanistic Psychology.**)

Library of Congress Catalog Card Number 80-81890
ISBN 0-89081-259-4

Foreword

Humanism is the most destructive force in our society today. And it is found everywhere, from medicine to coeducational sports. As Dr. Francis Schaeffer says, "All roads from Humanism lead to chaos. Humanism is not a builder, it is a destroyer."

Nowhere is that destructive power more apparent than in the field of education. Our once-great school system was originally built on the Christian concensus, with its roots in the northern European reformation thinking. For years the emphasis was on hard work, self-discipline, learning skills, self-sacrifice, and basic morality to achieve self-respect.

Today the emphasis is on sex, self-indulgence, government-supplied necessities, freedom of expression, etc., and has resulted in a drastic decline in learning skills.

The most dangerous of all college disciplines is the field of psychology. Freud and his humanistic disciples have taken over this academic discipline (that is studied by 85 percent of today's college students), and they use it to propagate the five basic doctrines of humanism:

1. atheism;
2. evolution;
3. amorality;
4. autonomous self-centered man;
5. socialist one-world view.

Every phase of psychology, whether Freudianism, Behaviorism, Skinnerism, or Transactional Analysis, is based on these erroneous assumptions. No wonder it is so harmful! Yet millions of Christians have been brainwashed into using these false concepts—in fact, some of these concepts are even taught favorably in Christian colleges.

Nelson E. Hinman has not been deceived by psychological jargon. He realizes that it is 180 degrees in opposition to biblical truth. I hope this book is just the first of many that will come off the press to unmask humanistic psychology for the hoax it really is.

We need to get back to the truths of Scripture and away from the fables of Freud that have led to so much counseling chaos. The Bible has the answers to the problems of life, but if people won't accept them they go to humanistic psychology for its supposed cures. But like the woman who had ''spent all she had on doctors and was nothing better'' until she came to Jesus, even so the doctors of humanism have little to offer. They can't even help themselves: psychiatrists still have the highest suicide rate in the country!

Man is a unique creature of God, and until psychologists recognize that fact they will never be able to solve man's inner problems.

Tim LaHaye
Author, Minister, Educator

Preface

This book has the potential of starting a revolution. It is a daring expose of humanism. In my view, the ever-creeping tentacles of humanism have had entirely too much status and utilization in Christian circles. This work by Nelson Hinman uncovers the unbiblical nature of humanistic psychology. With Bible in hand he carefully ferrets through the origins and development of secular philosophies that are regarded as "gospel" by the mainstream of students and scholars who study the nature of man. He skillfully uncovers the error of their ways. Nelson Hinman agrees with my friend, Dr. Henry Brandt, that God's Word—the Bible—is the only reliable guide for counseling, which leads to the growing idea that an effective counselor must be at least an amateur theologian and reasonably conversant with biblical principles.

At the heart of Nelson Hinman's thesis is that all truth is God's truth. In the eyes of the world the directness of Scripture regarding truth is an overwhelming problem. For example, the all-encompassing statement of John 17:17, "Thy Word is truth," is incomprehensible to humanistic thought. The idea that we must measure every detail of life, including the intellectual disciplines, in the light of Scripture completely short-circuits the mental processes of the average secularist.

It is unrealistic, of course, to expect man-centered men to conform to bibliocentric principles of evaluating psychology or any other area of life through the eyes of God as revealed in His Word. Godly men, however, who look at life through spiritual eyes should be able to study the nature and needs of man in a godly way. The genius of this book is centered in that basic purpose.

I urge the wide distribution of this valuable work by Nelson Hinman. It is appropriate reading by a large segment of the Christian community, especially those who are Christian counselors and others who are otherwise Christian leaders.

Dr. Paul A. Kienel,
Executive Director

Associated Christian
Schools International

CONTENTS

1

People and Positions

In reading this book it is important to carefully distinguish between people and positions. In this work all people are classified in one of two ways: *Christian* or *non-Christian*. There is no neutral class. And when positions are mentioned, only non-Christian and Christian concepts are in view. It is recognized that 1) a Christian may have non-Christian concepts mingled with his Christian beliefs, and 2) a non-Christian may hold to certain Christian concepts in his world view.

For example, a non-Christian may believe that marriage is intended to be a permanent relationship. This doesn't make him a Christian, but in this area his thinking is correct. It is a biblical position. In a similar way, a Christian may believe in humanistic evolution but at the same time have true faith in Jesus Christ as his only hope of eternal life. His position on salvation is unassailable. But his position on evolution is open to criticism. If one attacks a person's non-Christian position, one must be careful not to attack the person's integrity as an individual.

No believer, even after many years of study, knows all that can be known. Although the Christian has the true key to all knowledge necessary to life (2 Peter 1:3,4 and 2 Timothy 3:16,17), nevertheless he still sees "through a glass darkly." In most areas of available knowledge, he only knows in part. Not until we see Christ face-to-face will we know fully, as we are known (1 Corinthians 13:12).

We cannot, therefore, hold a slack, indifferent attitude

toward obtaining further knowledge. We are to study to show ourselves approved by God, and press on to know Him who has called us out of darkness into His marvelous light.

Neither can we be passive about error. We must be prepared to refute every speculative position and system of thought that exalts itself against the knowledge of God (2 Corinthians 10:5). But in doing so we must not tear down speculative *people*. We *must* distinguish between people and their positions.

One further clarification needs to be made. It may appear that this work is attacking all psychology. This is not so.

I am well aware that secular psychology has made many important contributions to humanity, especially in learning tools and in teaching processes. Most educated people have been taught more effectively and learned more rapidly because of the findings of psychologists. Industrial workers are more efficient, and they labor in less-oppressive conditions for the same reason. Because of psychological research, stutterers can overcome an embarrassing disability, sleep-loss damage can be identified and corrected, and thought processes can be improved. Child developmental stages are better understood, and adolescent problems are less baffling because of the work of psychological experimentation.

Many other contributions to human welfare have been made because psychologists have studied deviant behavior, physiological dysfunctions, and psychosomatic difficulties. In other words, in the laboratory the experimental work of psychology has been (and may continue to be) quite valuable. Some great, dedicated, serious-minded people are deeply involved in such work. There is much that they can still do. I applaud them.

But when a counselor believes that mankind is the product of animalistic, evolutionary processes rather than the creation of God, made in His own likeness and image, his counsel will be affected accordingly. He cannot consider man's true purpose in life because he does not know what it is. He cannot understand that man is intended to live in loving fellowship with his Creator and his neighbor. Neither can he understand the high moral absolutes that man is designed to maintain, or the damage that inevitably results when man violates those standards. As these counselors look at man, instead of saying with Hamlet, "How like a god he is," they say with Skinner and other behaviorists, "How like an animal, how like a pigeon, how like a rat, man is." This is because their presuppositions and their processes are rooted in error.

Still worse, these counselors do not know that the Creator has given an Instruction Manual by which man must live, or that it contains the methodology by which man is to be corrected when he fails. Of course I am referring to the Bible. The counselor who ignores the principles, rules, regulations, and other data in this Instruction Manual will jeopardize his counselee more often than he will help him. I have personally dealt with hundreds of people who for this reason have been devastated, disillusioned, and discouraged.

Imagine a surgeon who, lacking any electronic skills, attempts to repair a breakdown in an intricate computer system. He will not succeed. In fact, he will do no good at all, unless accidentally. Furthermore, he risks increasing the computer's damage if he gets seriously involved in adjusting its circuitry. The problem is not that he is a poor surgeon; he may be the best. The problem is that he is *out of his field*. He is trying to do something about which he is totally ignorant. Computers need electronic technicians, not surgeons.

For a psychologist to offer counsel while failing to acknowledge the Creator's design or to follow His instructions is to run a far greater risk. A psychologist must know the design and purpose of the life he wants to mend, and he must know it thoroughly. Moreover, he will be more effective if he possesses and understands how to use the Designer's Instruction Manual. Above all, he should have an intimate, personal knowledge of the Creator-Designer. The best possible help that a counselor can have is that of the Creator Himself when dealing with one of His troubled creatures.

2

Survey of the Problem

Psychology is a study of human beings. It is an attempt to determine who and what they are, why they behave as they do, and what happens to them as a result of their behavior.

Could there be a more interesting subject? Probably not. For nothing is more interesting to any person than knowledge about himself. For example, consider the following questions.

Who am I? Am I someone important? Is there any value, anything significant or honorable, about me? Is there any knowable purpose for my life?

What am I? An animal? A living machine? A product of an evolutionary process? Or am I a created being?

Is my life predetermined? Am I controlled by forces external or internal that are beyond my choice or control? Can I control my life regardless of my environment or my nature?

These questions, and countless others similar to them, are not only interesting but vitally important. Accurate or inaccurate answers to such questions may determine whether one is a happy, well-adjusted, peaceful, successful person with a grip on his future, or whether he is a miserable, defeated, hopeless, helpless victim of impersonal forces of "blind fate."

Psychology deals with these and other similar questions. And they are vital questions. Many people search earnestly within themselves for an understanding of human nature and the answers to such questions as these. But potential dangers lurk there. Note what one college professor has said: "The study of psychology is a dangerous thing." With this thought, Gerald H. O'Donnell, Assistant Professor of Psychology at

Nyack College (Nyack, New York), introduces his study guide for a class called "Psychology in a Christian Prospective."

Professor O'Donnell explains his meaning by adding, "for in making man the focal point of our investigation and reflection, we face certain risks that are not present in other types of scientific study.

> For one thing, whenever we try to examine ourselves, our study is always tainted by self-deception. It seems that we simply lack the courage and candidness to see ourselves as we really are. This tendency toward self-deception is apparent even in the most elementary attempts at self-evaluation, in which we readily confuse what we are with what we would like to be, and tend to become so enamored over the few virtues and talents that we possess, that we blind ourselves to even our most blatant weaknesses and faults. Man's tendency to see life through rose-colored glasses is greatest when he looks at himself.

The danger lies in man's disposition to self-deception. What standards will he use? Will he compare himself with others? Paul the Apostle, writing to the people of Corinth, states:

> We dare not make ourselves of the number, or compare ourselves with some, that commend themselves; but they, measuring themselves by themselves, and comparing themselves among themselves, are not wise (2 Corinthians 10:12).

The Amplified Bible translates the last two clauses of that verse even more emphatically: "When they measure themselves with themselves and compare themselves with one another, they are without understanding and behave unwisely."

In other words, it is foolish to judge oneself by comparison with other human beings. Paul said we "dare not" do this. He considered it hazardous to do so. The only safe alternative is to use the Word of God as the standard of measurement. That is the *only* way to make honest self-evaluation. It may not provide a "good self-image," but it will provide an *accurate* one.

Dr. William Pickthorn, a Bible teacher for over 30 years (who at one time was connected with Stanford University), agrees heartily with Professor O'Donnell. Now retired from Bethany Bible College of Santa Cruz, Dr. Pickthorn believes that psychology is peculiarly and particularly dangerous to those who are unaware of the fact that (humanistic) psychology is fallen man's study of himself without being aware that he is fallen. He went on to say, "Even if they are aware of the fall of man, secular psychologists rarely, if ever, understand what that implies. So it is quite often a case of the blind leading the blind, and both falling into the ditch of unbelief." Psychology, as it is studied today in almost all of our colleges, whether secular or sacred, is based on wrong presuppositions.

Let's take a look at this word "presupposition." What does it have to do with psychology? Isn't psychology supposed to be a study of *facts?* Yes, but there are always theories about what those facts mean. Take the fact of man's existence. There can be no real argument about whether or not he exists. There he is. That's a fact. But—where did he come from? Was he created? Or did he evolve from some lower form of life? What was the initial source of life? Did it come from God, or did it just happen? And on, and on, and on!

In the search for truth, the answers to such questions are generally tainted by the preconceived beliefs or disbeliefs of the searcher. What he expects to find is generally what he does find. Those beliefs are presuppositions. All scientists and researchers start with them. Note what Abraham Kuyper, in his "Lectures on Calvinism," said about this: "Every science, in a certain degree, starts from faith. . . . Every science presupposes faith in self, in our self-consciousness; presupposes faith in the accurate working of our senses; presupposes faith in the correctness of the laws of thought; presupposes faith in something universally hidden behind the special phenomena; presupposes faith in life; and especially, presupposes faith in the principles from which we proceed; which signifies that all these indispensible axioms, needed in a scientific investigation do not come to us by proof, but are established in our judgment by our inner conception and given with our self-consciousness."

Note Mr. Kuyper's use of the idea of self *"faith in self"*; *"in our self-consciousness,"* *"our senses,"* *"our judgment."* He is correct. Man tends to believe in his self-powers. This is not bad unless man behaves as if he is autonomous, which means that he recognizes no law higher than himself. Such a self-oriented person denies any absolute authority. He rejects God. There is no room in his thinking for either God or His Word. This is a perilous condition.

But God's Word says, "The reverent and worshipful fear of the Lord is the beginning and the principle and choice part of knowledge—that is, its starting point and its essence; but fools despise skillful and godly wisdom, instruction and discipline (Proverbs 1:7 Amplified Bible).

The beginning of knowledge, its principle and choice part, is *worshipful reverence for God.* This is the only true foundation of knowledge, the one solid place on which all truth stands. Everything else, even heaven and earth, shall pass away, but God's Word will stand forever.

What shall we say, then, when a psychology has been developed by men who do not believe that man is a created being, made in the likeness and image of his Creator, and who do not understand that man has violated his Creator's law, thus spoiling that image and damaging that likeness? The conclusions of any investigation ignoring these premises are certainly open to challenge. A Bible believer need not accept any psychology that ignores or refuses to fully consider this thesis.

Back to presuppositions: Man has a particularly difficult job admitting to himself that his presuppositions may be wrong. On the contrary, he will often go to unreasonable lengths to avoid anything that may contradict them. Man is never so great a salesman as when he tries to convince himself of the validity of his presuppositions. If he has a greater skill, it is his ability to ignore whatever contradicts his prejudices.

There is now a strong move afoot to develop a true, Bible-based, Christ-centered psychology. Dr. Jay Adams, Dr. Henry

Brandt, and Dr. Larry Crabb (to name a few among many) are producing books that are creating a revolution in this area. The National Association of Nouthetic Counselors is organized and dedicated to the same goals. At least two foundations are dedicated to establishing the theme that the Scriptures are an all-sufficient source of information on the cause and correction of man's spiritual, mental, and emotional problems. They are the Christian Counseling and Educational Foundation in Philadelphia and the Bible Counseling Foundation in Washington, D.C. A third one is in the process of being formed. It is the Highlands Biblical Counseling Foundation in San Bruno, California.

However, most (if not all) systematic, scientific (so-called) approaches to psychology consider humanity's existence to be the result of animalistic, evolutionary processes. Note the words of Hilgard and Atkinson in their introductory psychology test:

> Man is a flesh-and-blood organism related to other organisms through an evolutionary history. Man's habits, thoughts, and aspirations are centered in his brain and nervous system, and whenever we study him, we study something he does or expresses through his bodily processes. We may examine a man as a vertebrate, a mammal, and a primate—as one who shares an evolutionary background with the rest of the biological world.[1]

These authors merely assume the validity of their reasoning. They have not proven it; they have accepted it as true by faith, and by faith alone. The accuracy of the data used to teach evolution has been seriously challenged. The bibliography of contra-evolution literature is impressive. A brief, selected list of such books has been included for those interested in pursuing this theme.

As Christians, we must be quick to admit that it is also by

---

1. *Introduction to Psychology,* 4th edition (Harcourt, Brace and World, 1967), p. 30.

faith that we accept the validity of the Genesis account of man's origin. But while evolutionists insist on their own right to have faith in their assumptions, they deny the Christian the same right to his faith, saying he is foolish while they are wise. The sophistry must be rejected. The Christian faith is far more reasonable than theirs.

When the evolutionist's story is compared to the Bible account, properly presented (as Francis A. Schaeffer has done in *Genesis in Space and Time*), [2] it is apparent that the Bible story is by far the more credible explanation of man's existence. As Dr. Schaeffer so often insists, "the Bible is not exhaustive truth, but it is true truth." It always stands, undamaged by its enemies' attacks, when it is permitted to speak for itself.

It is impossible to accept as true both the biblical account of the origin of man and the one cited above by Hilgard and Atkinson. One of the two theories must be wrong, and we must choose between them.

Right here lies a serious danger, as indicated by Gerald O'Donnell and William Pickthorn in the opening of this chapter. If a Christian accepts the humanistic position (that man is the result of an evolutionary process and was not created in the likeness and image of God) he is permitting impurity into his beliefs about man, about the Bible, and ultimately about God Himself. Uncorrected, such an impurity is like a bit of leaven that will eventually "leaven the whole lump" of that person's relationship with God. It opens the door to further error.

In exactly this way, untold thousands of Christian young people are accepting information that will result in the destruction of their faith in the Bible, unless it is quickly corrected.

No one can syncretize humanism and the Word of God without corrupting it. They are antithetical. Blending them is like trying to mix light and darkness, a process that only dims

___

2. Regal Books, S/L Publications and InterVarsity Press, 1977.

the light. The darkness must go, and it will go, when the light is permitted to shine in its purity. This will be more thoroughly discussed later in this book.

To have a scripturally based presupposition for psychology, must acknowledge that man was created in the likeness and image of God. Therefore, to know all that can be known about man, we must know all we can about God. To know all that can be known about God, we must know about Jesus Christ, for He is the truth about God, and the way to God. If we are to know all that we can about Jesus Christ, we must know the Bible, for it is the greatest authoritative source of information about Him.

As mentioned, the absence of such a body of teaching is apparent. The lack of such literature has prompted the writing of this book. However, it should be obvious to the serious-minded student that a book of this type cannot cover the entire science of psychology. To do so would require many volumes and greater knowledge than this author possesses. But there are three or four things that this book should accomplish.

First, it should alert new students of psychology to the fact that most psychology taught today clashes with the Bible at many points. Second, it should help these students to learn to identify the humanistic factors that will constantly appear in their "psych" courses. Third, it should awaken many people to the fact that the Scriptures are all-sufficient for all things that pertain to life and godliness, as Peter has written:

> According as his divine power hath given unto us all things that pertain unto life and godliness through the knowledge of him that hath called us to glory and virtue, whereby are given to us exceeding great and precious promises, that by these ye might be partakers of the divine nature, having escaped the corruption that is in the world through lust. (2 Peter 1:3,4)

And fourth, it is the prayer of this author that this work will inspire many young persons to pursue careers in psychology and earn the credentials to qualify them to write and publish material based upon truly biblical presuppositions. The time has come for such books to receive wide acceptance.

3

What Humanism Is

Humanism and Christianity are incompatible. They oppose each other at critical points, and it is impossible to reconcile these differences. Some of these conflicting beliefs are clearly seen when set in parallel columns:

Humanism	Christianity
1. Rejects the Bible as a rule and guide for life's values and behavior.	Accepts the Bible as the only rule and guide for life's values and behavior.
2. Denies the existence of a personal God.	Rests solidly on the existence of a personal God.
3. Believes that man is competent to solve his life problems without supernatural assistance.	Believes that man is wholly unable to solve his basic life problems without God-given assistance.
4. Teaches that man is autonomous, a law unto himself.	Teaches that God is sovereign and that man is obligated to obey Him.
5. Encourages self-exaltation and self-love.	Requires self-denial, love of God, and love of one's neighbor.
6. Focuses man's attention on helping himself.	Focuses man's attention on helping others.
7. Is totally self-oriented.	Is totally Christ-oriented.

There are many sub-items of conflict between advocates of humanism and champions of Christianity not discussed in this book, but the above will establish the principle conflicting areas. When the word "self" predominates, one should be alert to possible departures from true biblical teaching. It is not always so, but generally a "selfism" is a red flag indicating the presence of humanisms.

Not all "self" words are objectionable. For example, self-denial and self-examination are recommended procedures in the Bible, but self-righteousness and selfishness are condemned. The Bible admits that people love themselves, but never advocates the practice. In fact, self-love is identified with perilous times and is at the head of a long list of things from which to turn away:

> This know also, that in the last days perilous times shall come. For men shall be lovers of their own selves, covetous, boasters, proud, blasphemers, disobedient to parents, unthankful, unholy, without natural affection, truce-breakers, false accusers, incontinent, fierce, despisers of those that are good, traitors, heady, high-minded, lovers of pleasure more than lovers of God; having a form of godliness, but denying the power thereof: from such turn away (2 Timothy 3:1-5).

The subject of self-love will be covered more thoroughly in Chapter 10.

Humanism is an avowed enemy of Christianity. In the preface to The Humanist Manifestos I and II (published by Prometheus Books, Buffalo, N.Y.) it is stated, ". . . as in 1933, humanists still believe that traditional theism, especially faith in the prayer-hearing God, assumed to love and care for persons, to hear and understand their prayers, and to be able to do something about them, is an unproved and outmoded faith. Salvationism, based on mere affirmation, still appears as harmful, diverting people to a false hope of heaven hereafter. Reasonable minds look to other means for survival. . . ."

This is unmitigated blasphemy. Yet there is more, as the book continues:

> Using technology wisely, we can control our environment, conquer poverty, markedly reduce disease, extend our life-span, significantly modify our behavior, alter the course of human evolution and cultural development, unlock vast new powers, and provide humankind with unparalleled opportunity for achieving an abundant and meaningful life. . . .

Having done away with a personal God that answers prayer and offers salvation, the humanists exalt man to a cocksure position, able to give the human race all it needs for a rich, full life. They would dethrone Jesus Christ, who came that we might have life and have it more abundantly (John 10:10), and enthrone their own "saviors" to do the job of providing life abundantly for mankind.

Speaking about religion, *The Humanist Manifesto II* says two things:

> First: . . . We find insufficient evidence for belief in the existence of a supernatural; it is either meaningless or irrelevant to the question of survival and fulfillment of the human race. As non-theists, we begin with humans not God, nature not deity. . . . We can discover no divine purpose or providence for human species. While there is much that we do not know, humans are responsible for what we are or will become. No diety will save us: we must save ourselves.

> Second: Promises of immortal salvation or fear of eternal damnation is both illusory and harmful. They distract humans from present concerns, from self-actualization, and from rectifying social injustices. Modern science discredits such historic concepts as the "ghost in the machine" and the "separable soul." Rather, science af-

firms that the human species is an emergence from natural human evolutionary forces. . . . There is no credible evidence that life survives the death of the body. We continue to exist in our progeny and in the way that our lives have influenced others in our culture.

It would be difficult to find a more concise, blatant renunciation of the message of the Bible and the God of the Bible.

Humanism is not without organization. In 1896, the Ethical Union was founded to federate humanist secular societies then in existence. In 1899 they launched the Rationalist Press, but both remained quite small. However, in the mid-twentieth century, as humanism became more popular, the Ethical Union and Rationalist Press merged and became the British Humanist Association (1963), which was linked to the International Humanist. These bits of information are taken from Os Guinness' book *The Dust of Death,* published by InterVarsity Press.

In that same book, Mr. Guinness quotes Sir Julian Huxley: "Today, in twentieth-century man, the evolutionary process is at last becoming conscious of itself. . . . Human knowledge, worked over by human imagination, is seen as the basis to human understanding and belief, and the ultimate guide to human progress."

Keep in mind that while the humanists are seeking a better life for humanity, God's Word explains how to find that life. Humanists say that life worth living is found in self-actualization, self-confidence, self-acceptance, self-image theories, self-love, self-worth, and numerous other self-emphases. But God's Word says that to strive to save or to love one's own life is a sure way to lose it (Matthew 10:39 and John 12:25).

He that findeth his life shall lose it, and he that loseth his life for my sake shall find it (Matthew 10:39).
He that loveth his life and shall lose it, and he that hateth life in this world shall keep it unto life eternal (John 12:25).

According to Jesus, the way to find abundant life, to find out what and who you really are, to discover your full potential, is to take up your cross daily, deny your self, lose yourself in serving others, and follow Him. Then, and only then, will you discover life as God would have it lived.

4

What Humanism Does

Humanism is not a "Johnny-come-lately" concept. It has been with us from the beginning. A one-line definition of humanism could be that it is the belief that man is the center of the universe and is autonomous. This last word is a combination of two Greek words: *autos*, which means "self," and *nomos*, which means "law." Thus to be autonomous is to be a law unto one's own self, to be the author and enforcer to laws that concern one's self.

Another way to describe humanism as it is used in this book is to say that it is man's usurpation of the privileges and prerogative that belong to God alone. It is an invasion of God's right to rule His own creation. It is making one's own self to be his own God. It is putting too much emphasis on what self wants, with too little concern about what God wants.

Humanism has been around for a long time. Actually it started with Adam and Eve in the Garden of Eden. God has told them that the earth was theirs. They were to subdue and have dominion over it. As to the Garden itself, they were to tend it and have access to the fruit of all the trees for food, except for one tree.

In effect God had said, "Now as to our relationship, Adam and Eve—I have prepared a wonderful life for you both. But it requires total obedience for you to experience the wonder of it. But it is not difficult to obey. In fact, I will consider you to be thoroughly obedient and satisfactorily cooperative if you merely refrain from eating of the fruit of that one tree in the center of the Garden. We will call that one the Tree of Knowledge of Good and Evil.

"What I am saying to you, Adam, is that I do not want either you or Eve to get the knowledge of the difference between good and evil by experimentation. I want you to take my word for it. There is a tremendous difference between good and evil, but the day you learn that difference by experimentation, instead of knowing it by believing what I am telling you, a process of death will set in, and you shall surely die."

We know the rest of the story.

Eve was tempted to disobey, to take matters into her own hands. Her temptation was strong. Her deception was complete and she ate the fruit.

Next she took some to Adam, told him what she had done, and offered the forbidden fruit to him. Adam, fully aware of what he was doing, and not at all deceived, deliberately disobeyed. He chose to ignore God's warning. He too ate the forbidden fruit.

And, just as God had said, a *process of death* began. Adam and Eve began to die.

To comprehend this is difficult because the phenomenon of death is so common to us we do not see the dreadful factors involved.

Another fact that keeps us from grasping what happened to Adam and Eve is our failure to understand what spiritual death is. The Bible (1 Timothy 5:6) speaks of those who live in pleasure as being dead while they live. In Matthew 8:22 Jesus said, "let the dead bury their dead." In other words, let the spiritually dead bury their physically dead. There are other references to two kinds of death:

Verily, verily, I say unto you, He that heareth my word and believeth on him that sent me, hath everlasting life, and shall not come into condemnation, but is pleased from death unto life.

Verily, Verily, I say unto you, The hour is coming, and now is, when the dead shall hear the voice of the Son of

God, and they that hear shall live.

For as the Father hath life in himself, so hath he given to the Son to have life in Himself,

And hath given him authority to execute judgment also, because he is the Son of man.

Marvel not at this, for the hour is coming in which all that are in the graves shall hear his voice,

And shall come forth: they that have done good, unto the resurrection of life; and they that have done evil, unto the resurrection of damnation (John 5:24-29).

And you hath he quickened, who were dead in trespasses and sins. Even when we were dead in sins, he hath quickened us together with Christ (by grace ye are saved) (Ephesians 2:1,5).

And you, being dead in your sins and the uncircumcision of your flesh, hath he quickened together with him, having forgiven you all trespasses (Colossians 2:13).

We know that we have passed from death unto life, because we love the brethren. He that loveth not his brother abideth in death (1 John 3:14).

It is obvious that it was in the realm of spiritual death that God's warning to Adam and Eve began to take place. Notice the progression of evidence of spiritual death taking possession of them.

First shame, a new experience, entered their lives. Until they took matters into their own hands, they had not noticed that they were naked. Afterwards they did notice. They tried to cover up.

Then another new element followed their decision to be autonomous; fear, with its pulse-quickening, muscle-tensing stress, caused them to flee when they heard God's voice. Formerly that voice was a call to fellowship—to happy, friendly conversation. But this time it brought terror and panic to Adam, and he ran away to hide.

Sin not only brought shame and fear, but it caused mankind to act stupidly. Did Adam really think he could hide from God? Maybe not, but he would try.

Caught red-handed, Adam tried to shift the blame to his wife: "She gave it to me," He indirectly involved God in his disobedience, for he said to God, "the woman *You* gave me—she's to blame. You told me it wasn't good for me to be alone; You said she would be good for me. Now look at what happened to me." Adam was willing for Eve to take the blame that he faced. Maybe he could escape.

Adam's guilt is obvious. To his guilt, shame, and fear was added foolish conduct. Also, judgment settled down like a plague on all that pertained to him. His blessings turned to curses. Even the earth resisted his efforts by bringing forth thistles and thorns along with the fruit of his labor (Genesis 3:17-19). Neither Adam nor Eve was the same as before their sin. Nor was the world the same. Everything was damaged, changed. God's whole creation was altered and has remained under God's curse ever since.

Interpersonal problems developed in Adam's family. Anger, evil living (see 1 John 3:12) and eventually murder disrupted the home of Adam and Eve (Genesis 4:1-8). Cain, standing over the bloody, battered body of his brother, grimly portrays the horror and havoc that can develop when man takes matters into his own hands. Cain failed to take God's Word seriously and did what he wanted to do even though doing it violated God's commands. That is humanism as it is discussed in this book.

As it was then, so it is now. Whenever man decides that he is autonomous, his own legislator, his own policeman, his own judge and jury, he will sooner or later discover to his own sorrow that he has automatically become his own executioner. To his own dismay he learns that he is unable to stave off the penalty—he too "surely dies."

The horror of spiritual death leads to physical death. So we read of Adam (Genesis 5:5)—". . . and he died." Created in the likeness and image of God, Adam in the end could not possibly have looked like or been less like God. He became a human corpse, no longer a living being. Such is the penalty of sin, the fruit of humanism.

Another thing needs to be said about what happened to Adam. The result of his sin was not entirely judicial, as is the case when a son is spanked by a father for disobedience. It is more like a factual story in which I was slightly involved as a young boy. My chum and I were playing with a pair of carbide-gas miner's lamps. These lamps, attached to a cap, were worn by miners in a small coal mine near where I lived. No matter which way the miner's head was turned, the gas flame lighted the area directly in front of him.

My chum's father caught him wearing a lighted lamp near some open containers of gasoline. The father was furious as well as frightened. He severely reprimanded the lad, warning him loudly and at length about the danger of this action. But the boy forgot. He was having too much fun playing with the lamp. He carelessly leaned over a small pan of dirty gasoline, and got too close. A violent explosion occurred, engulfing the boy in flames. He lived, miraculously or tragically, depending on one's viewpoint, but he was horribly disfigured for life.

The pain and disfigurement were not the work of the father. They were the direct result of the son's disobedience. The father was not even responsible for the presence of the gasoline. The boy's failure to obey was the real fault.

It was a matter of cause and effect. The cause was not merely the lighted lamp. The boy's disobedience was added to the peril of the lamp's flame. The unheeded warning brought gasoline vapor and fire too close together. A violent explosion was the result. The effect was a hideously disfigured body. In a similar fashion, Adam's disobedience was *his* ruin. Such is the inevitable result of unpardoned disobedience.

Most people seem to think that what happened to Adam and Eve can only happen in a religious setting in direct rebellious confrontation with God. Few people seem to realize how widespread such humanism really is, how fully it has penetrated into every phase of man's life. It dominates philosophy. It is expressed in art. It is fundamental to the sciences, such as biology, zoology, sociology, geology, and psychology. It is heard in music. Worse yet, it dominates the new theology. Even more tragic is the fact that most marriages are built on humanistic foundations. It has spread like a plague into all but the purest of evangelical, biblical thinking.

Furthermore, our governmental processes are deeply affected by humanism's ignoring of God's absolute laws. Sociological goals are more important than moral issues to many of our politicians. A bureaucrat recently told a Christian lobby committee, "To us it makes no difference whether your god is a he, a she, or an it. We don't want to hear about it." This is sheer blasphemy and has no acceptable place in the government of any people. But it *is* a sign of the times in which we live.

The same new philosophy has shown up in our courts. A recent decision by a Northern California judge legalized marijuana based on what he thought was the popular public opinion rather than upon laws on the books of California's legal system. Sociological issues overruled the law.

The executive branch of our federal government recently went through an appalling scandal, and a president was forced to resign in disgrace. Even a cursory review of the sordid events that developed in this tragedy reveals the almost total substitution of personal vendetta in place of due process of law as bitterness and resentment, hatred and viciousness, lying and intrigue circumvented the courts and overruled the very laws that this department was sworn, by oath, to enforce. This is humanism on a rampage.

That whole unsavory affair is a great departure from the righteousness that exalts a nation. It is a solemn, vivid demonstration that sin is indeed a reproach to any people. Not only is sin a reproach, but it is death—not only to persons but also to a government.

The three branches of our government—executive, legislative, and judicial—have been infected by these trends, forcing us farther and farther away from the foundational absolutes of our constitution and from the immutable laws of God.

Humanism as it is defined in this book (autonomous humanity; self taking matters into its own hands; defying the absolutes of God's laws) has not only eaten away and thus weakened the strength of our government, but it also is infecting the morals of our whole social structure. It does this by flooding our way of life with humanistic-controlled television programs, movies, books, magazines, and newspapers.

An illustration of how this is possible can easily be seen in TV newscasts. We do not always see the news as it actually is —contrary to what our news anchormen and on-the-spot reporters tell us. We see a highly edited version of the news. Francis Schaeffer, vividly shows how this can happen in his film *How Should We Then Live?*

Dr. Schaeffer staged an act with skilled actors depicting a riot. Cameras were carefully placed and a script skillfully written. The resulting film was reported in such a manner that the "rioters" seemed wholly justified in their cause. The police were portrayed and their actions described in a manner that seemed to prove that police brutality was rampant.

Then, repositioning the cameras to different angles, the exact scene was redone by the same actors. This time the presentation and narration result was totally different from the first. Now the "rioters" were seen in a bad light and the law-enforcement agents were the "good guys." The same scene gave opposite results, depending on the desire of the director and the position of the cameras.

This is not intended to be a condemnation of our nation's newscasters. As far as this author is concerned, they are honest people striving to be objective and faithful to the facts. The above paragraphs are not written to prove that this actually happens in getting the news to the public. Instead, it points out that even honest men cannot guarantee that their work is free from error or bias, or uninfluenced by chance positions of cameras and crews. Neither can anyone really be certain that the policies of the networks, the presuppositions of the writers, and the social pressures of the day are not strong factors in presenting the news. It must be remembered that there are many possible variations in gathering, editing, and presenting the news. Chance plus time plus temperament plus opportunity cannot guarantee unbiased accuracy.

Suppose a situation were to develop in which a troubled government wanted to shift the emphasis from democracy to dictatorship. With contrived secrecy, an elite group of intellectuals, properly financed, could begin to manipulate the public's thinking by improper use of the news media, especially television. Since the vividness of pictorial presentations gives the viewer the realism afforded to an eyewitness with "you-are-there" feeling, most people could be led to believe anything such an elite group would choose to present. Add that to the power of the printed page and the potential is frightening. We could become a manipulated and controlled people.

This is not a doomsday tolling of bells. Rather, it is an attempt to make a clarion challenge to youth to see frontiers of usefulness in reversing a trend of the times and reestablishing God's absolutes as guidelines for our society.

This frontier of usefulness is great and offers amazing opportunities to live significant, meaningful lives in this social structure. Consider what a vast field of useful, purposeful, exciting careers are available in the background of the entertainment media: TV, radio, movies, stage shows, plays, operas, musical presentations of all sorts. I am not talking about becoming entertainers. I am talking about reversing the fact that these things are being used as vehicles for the spread of these humanisms. Why cannot Christian youth invade this field as producers, writers, directors, editors, or whatever areas of activity will turn the tide?

By these media the authors and directors are able to present the views in the most forceful way possible in today's society. And all of this is done in the name of entertainment. The themes and plots of the plays and the movies, the lines of the jokes, the lyrics of the music, the costuming, the physical action of the actors and dancers are forceful beyond most of our comprehension as a method of molding the minds and lifestyle of the viewers.

Viewers of TV are generally in highly vulnerable attitudes for the reception of whatever message, good or bad, these authors and directors are trying to get across to them. The viewer is in a relaxed mood. He becomes emotionally involved, highly interested, and entertained. The medium he is exposed to has almost total access to his subconscious mind. His senses are passively, uncritically inactive as he watches and listens. He is being amused.

To muse is to think. But *amused* means to *not* think. The Greek prefix "a" is negative. The amused viewer has surrendered his thought processes to the medium he is involved with. It is thinking for him. He is unwittingly being programmed with the message of the author-director-producer behind the presentation unless he has learned to listen and view critically what is before him. Unless he identifies what is wrong and rejects it in his mind, he will be passively accepting it and eventually believing it, which in turn will make it part of his thinking. This will become a controlling factor in what he does in his life.

Not all that comes across in the entertainment field is planned to indoctrinate the audiences, but much of it is. Many directors and writers have publicly stated that they have a message to get across in their movies and TV productions. In this sense these people are philosophers trying to mold public opinion with their humanistic views. Therefore the entertainment field offers tremendous challenges for writers producers, and directors who are Christian and Bible-oriented to change the face of their world.

Not only the news and entertainment media offer opportunities for significant, useful, life-changing careers to halt humanism's spread; there is an even more fertile place to do so: It is the scholastic, educational system.

Here of all places is the greatest potential to turn the tide. Almost every discipline, from A to Z, including anthropology, zoology, philosophy, psychology, and sociology, is humanistically oriented. There is a great need for well-trained minds to be dedicated to a modern reformation, a rebirth of interest and belief in God's absolutes and the dethroning of human selfism.

The battle lines are clearly drawn. There are really only two sides: the kingdom of God and the kingdom of self. Outwardly it looks as if the humanistic forces will totally overwhelm the world, but Christians know better, for they have read the last chapter. They know that the kingdoms of this world will fall and God's kingdom will triumph.

It is important to be on the right side. Let all who ponder this remember that it is either one or the other. There is no middle ground.

5

Humanism and Self

In the past three decades since World War Two, a whole new literature has developed that can accurately be called a self-help literature. A visit to almost any bookstore will certify this. I am not referring to self-help books that teach gardening, cooking, and other manual skills. I am referring to the literature that aggrandizes the power of the human mind, books with titles like *The Magic of Believing*, *Psycho-Cybernetics*, *The Power of Positive Thinking*, the *Magic Power of Your Mind*, and myriads of others. A catalog of these titles would be difficult to develop and keep up-to-date, for the marketplace is being flooded with attempts to satisfy the public appetite for this philosophy.

I am not objecting to the trend. These authors—most of them—have caught a glimpse of what man is capable of doing and being. I have purchased and read many of these books with great pleasure and personal benefit. From them I have learned a lot about self-acceptance, self-reliance, self-image, and the potential power that is available to mankind. They teach that all one needs to do is believe, set goals, visualize, imagine, remove all doubt and negativism, to work, plan, and be enthusiastic—then success is certain. In this way of life there are no limits (except self-imposed ones) to what can be done, so they say.

The strange thing about all this is that this teaching actually works quite well. Not perfectly, but amazing things do happen to and for those who accept this as a way of life. Slowly, over a period of several years, I began to realize why it worked. It works because of the fact that God created things this way. Man was also designed to love his Creator, to walk with Him, and to love his neighbor as himself. However, these books seldom, if ever, mention this side of the matter. They aggrandize self, with almost total disregard for man's duty to God or his duty to his neighbor. Therefore man's self tends to be treated as if it were autonomous.

After years of involvement, I was shocked to discover that this type of literature was actually alienating me from the God I professed to serve. I began to be aware that may appetite for the Bible and for prayer had diminished dangerously. *Things* had become quite important to me—things like money, expensive cars, clothes, and houses. Fame, success, and fortune had become goals that I constantly visualized and sought for, and to some degree had attained.

It took a personal and painful tragedy to fully awaken me to what was really happening. I was wandering far from the fellowship with God that I had known so well for over 30 years. The return was slow and awkward. Overcoming and overthrowing the self that I had set upon the throne of my life wasn't easy. But God was faithful, and the return was eventually accomplished.

With fellowship resorted, with Jesus Christ again enthroned in my life, and with the Bible as my guide and rule, I started rebuilding a ministry and a life that had deteriorated sadly. Taking a true biblical attitude toward self, I began to find the proper balance between God's goals for me and my own self-established ones. I am more convinced than ever of man's potential for success. But I am keenly aware that gaining even the whole world is unprofitable if in the process I lose my right relationship to God. This latter is exactly the risk one takes when self becomes autonomous. That is why this self-help literature is dangerous.

I would like to be young enough to be able to see what could happen in a life where 1) a person had self totally subservient to Jesus Christ, 2) his neighbor's welfare was completely ahead of his own, 3) the Bible was his final authority in all his values, and 4) his heart was perfectly tuned to love and obey God. Maybe it is not too late for me, even at my age, to see this potential developed.

God's prophet wrote:

> The eyes of the Lord run to and fro throughout the whole earth to show himself strong in behalf of them whose heart is perfect toward Him (2 Chronicles 16:9).

I believe He had just such a person in mind. Personally speaking, I want to be that sort of person.

There is another type of self-literature that has become equally popular—maybe more so. I refer to Eric Berne's *Games People Play*, which sold over three millions copies. This book champions a self theory called Transactional Analysis (T.A.). Its design seems to be to develop autonomous adults. Again, it is self without God!

On the heels of Berne's success came Thomas Harris's book, *I'm O.K.—You're O.K.*, which is rooted in thinly disguised Freudianism and structured in the Transactional Analysis of Berne. This book sold over a million hardbook copies, and has been reprinted in a dozen paperback issues. Again, it is an exalting of self without God.

There are other modern books on psychological and psychiatric themes available—books by Abraham Maslow, Albert Ellis, William Glasser, O. Hobart Mowrer, and a host of others. They all have one thing in common: self is king. The personal God of the Bible is not acknowledged as an important force in their theories.

Since Sigmund Freud there has been no end of books on man and his problems. They still pour off the presses, and most are based on the presupposition THERE IS NO PERSONAL GOD.

To understand more fully the source of this not-God-but-self theory, we start with Thomas Aquinas (1225-74 A.D.). He is thought by many people to have been the outstanding theologian of his day. This thinking is still influential in some sections of Roman Catholic theology.

There are three things about Aquinas that demand our attention if if we really want to know how humanistic selfism has been able to spread so far. Selfism started in a theological error but fanned out into the Western world's philosophical thinking and eventually arrived into our times as an overwhelming flood.

The first thing we need to know about Aquinas is that in his studies of Adam and Eve's sin, called the fall of man, he decided that only man's *will* was damaged when sin entered human life. Man's *intellect,* he said, remained intact, undamaged, and still perfect. This helps us understand why Aquinas taught that man, out of his own resources, could search for, find, and classify all truth. This brilliant priest felt competent to do this perfectly by himself. He failed to realize that man was also in intellectual conflict with God—in short, in rebellion against the Creator.

The second thing we need to know is that Aquinas was captivated by the Greek philosophy of Aristotle, a man who knew only the mythical gods of the Greeks. He also had a great mind and a profound (although godless) theory of truth and the answers to life's problems. Aquinas became an Aristotelian thinker.

The third thing is that Aquinas did not differentiate between what the Bible taught about life, truth, and the answers to man's problems and what Aristotle taught. He syncretized the two. Thus came into existence a highly compounded error.

For a fuller, more scholarly treatment of the Aquinas error one should read Francis Schaeffer's books *How Should We Then Live?* and *Escape from Reason.*

Dante (1265-1320 A.D.), Petrarch (1304-71), Kant (1724-1804), Hegel (1770-1831), Kierkegaard (1833-55), plus the power of the printed page, plus the rise in availability of educational opportunities provided a steady flow of philosophic humanism into the Western world.

The Reformation almost turned the tide around, but the force of the Renaissance helped perpetuate the flood tide.

The message of man's autonomy was kept flowing by Darwin, Freud, Jung, Adler, the Huxleys, and many other influential people.

It reached its peak in Germany, flooded the European continent, spilled over into England, and by 1900 was infiltrating American colleges and universities, eventually infiltrating seminaries until today its branches have crawled into our pulpits and are accepted uncritically in many forms by many individual Christians.

It is interesting to note that our drug culture got its start in this humanistic philosophy. By rejecting God and the absolutes in His Bible, philosophers began running into dead-end thinking. Francis Schaeffer says that many of them began to believe that there was no absolute truth, no universal truth at all. Everything was relative and situational. If someone said something was true, someone else asked, "Compared to what?" "In what situation is it true?" This led further and further away from ultimate truth. God-is-dead theories developed. By that it is meant that the issue of whether there is a personal God became a dead issue.

Man was considered to be an animal—a highly intelligent one, but nevertheless an animal. The universe was considered a colossal machine. Some believed that man was a living machine, programmed like the universe.

So what's to live for? Nothing. Eat, drink, and be merry, for tomorrow comes Extinction.

Thus the thinkers concluded, "It's the end of man, too." B.F. Skinner said the extinction of man, as man, would be good riddance. In other words, man should not be thought of as different from an animal.

But the Huxleys said no. They believed that somehow, in man's mind, in his head, was either the truth or the way to the truth. They believed that if man could escape himself, escape his frustrations, get outside himself, he could find reality.

They recommended hallucinogenic drugs. Thus was born ''The-truth-is-in-one's-head'' thesis.

This theory said that one can open up his hand with drugs, take a trip into reality, to an ultimate experience—beyond reason—to an escape from futility and in this manner find truth. A drug culture was born.

At first it was an intellectual pursuit, but the intellectuals soon began to lose interest. However a new culture was ready to pick it up. The rock groups sent this theme all over the Western world. This drug scene was here to stay. Just how deeply it has penetrated our culture is graphically told by Paul Harvey in one of his columns, where he pointed out that over one-third of America's 37 million school children regularly use drugs of some kind.

This has been a brief look into how humanism has infected our society. It is here to stay. It won't die out or go away on its own. Every young person who lives to normal maturity will have to face this ugly fact and make some determination about how he will live with it.

As seen elsewhere in this book, these humanistic ideas come at us from many directions via TV, movies, books, popular music, newspapers, and magazines. Humanism is in our schools. It is in our churches. We can't escape it, but we can reject it. We must oppose it.

We are not left to the merciless pressures of Satan's kingdom. Christ, who is truth personified, has promised us a truth that will make us free. God's Word is truth and can be hidden in our hearts (Psalm 119:11) to keep us from sinning against God. All who are willing to do His will can know the truth and thus be free from the tragic consequences of humanism.

6

The Debut
of Psychology

Where does psychology fit into this humanistic trend? Up until this point humanistic *philosophy* has been discussed, with very little said about humanistic *psychology*.

Compared to philosophers, psychologists are a new breed. The latter have been with us about a hundred years. Philosophers, however, were in the world before New Testament times. The Apostle Paul on Mars Hill (Acts 17:18 ff.) had an encounter with some of them; they were no less hostile to Christianity than some modern philosophers are today. To them Paul seemed to be a "babbler" (v. 18). The history of the Greek word translated "babbler" is interesting and informative. It helps us understand what the ancient philosophers thought about Christianity. The word is *spermalogos*. *Smerma* means "seed," *Logos* means an "expression of thought." Primarily, *spermalogos* is an adjective, but in slang it was used as a noun signifying a crow, or other bird, picking up seeds. Eventually it came to refer to a man who picked up scraps that fell from loads, hence a parasite, who lived at the expense of others. Later it was used to describe a man who picked up scraps of information and, as a plagiarist, made merchandise of this secondhand knowledge. It also described a person who made a show, in unscientific style, of knowledge obtained through misunderstanding lectures. It insinuated that the person it described was ignorant, having only erroneous information.

Thus the word "babbler" labeled Paul and his message as a fool spouting forth foolishness.

It would be unfair to ignore the fact that although the majority of the philosophers on Mars Hill that day did contemptuously sneer at and reject both Paul and his message, nevertheless a few became followers of the apostle and believed. Acts 17:34 names two of these new believers.

In Colossians 2:8 Paul speaks of philosophy, warning that it can be deceptive when it depends on humanistic tradition and the basic principles of this world instead of on Christ. I do not take this as a denunciation of all philosophy. However, it points out sharply that when studying philosophy one must be wary if it neglects and rejects Jesus Christ.

Dr. Charles S. Price was an eloquent, highly effective evangelist in the 1920s and the 1930s. His doctorate was earned at Oxford in the field of philosophy. I once said to him when he was a guest in my home, "Doctor Price, the studies you have in philosophy must have been a great help to you."

He replied, "On the contrary, it was a formidable barrier between me and God as He is portrayed in the Bible. I was totally unable to believe both what the philosophers taught and what the Bible taught about Him. That was my main problem. I had to choose between what I had spent over a dozen years learning and what the Bible had to say. I had, up until my conversion to Christ, completely rejected the Bible.

"No," he went on, "philosophy was not a help; it was a hindrance, a serious one."

Philosophy and its proponents were in the world before the New Testament era, and in general, they were contemptuous enemies of Christianity. To more accurately pinpoint how long philosophers have been around, we note that Pythagoras, six centuries before Christ, was the first man who called himself a philosopher. What he meant by that is not clear, for it was not until Plato's time (428-348 B.C.) that the word had specialized or technical usage ("love of wisdom and truth"). Originally the word was applied to one who studied any subject—music, math, language, or whatever—somewhat like the degree "Ph.D." is given in many disciplines today.

Socrates (470-399 B.C.) and Plato were contemporaries. Both were philosophers. Socrates is one of the first to narrow the field of philosophic studies to concentrate on universal truths about human conduct and character. This field of study is actually the seed-plot out of which came (much later) what we know today as psychology.

Psychology has one of its roots deep in the soil of philosophy. We need to be aware that philosophy became influenced by a way of thinking called "empiricism." Originally the Empiricists were from one of three schools of medicine in Greco-Roman times. These people were skeptical of all theoretical explanations unless the theories could be demonstrated in laboratory fashion to the human senses.

Empirical thinking began to dominate almost all philosophy. In its extreme form it championed knowledge that came from sense experience in contrast to that derived from reason and logic. This eventually became the banner of scientific research. By the early 1800s it was generally accepted that man could know only that which was discernible by the five senses: seeing, smelling, touching, hearing, and tasting. In other words, unless a thing had substance that was measurable and definable, it did not exist except as an imaginary object.

Thus was developed the theory that there was no nonphysical reality. Dualistic thinking about man having a mind (or a soul) and a body was seriously challenged. Since the mind or soul was not open to investigation (by empirical standards), their existence was denied. This did not prove that nonexistence of nonmaterial parts in man, but it did establish a *world view*, a *presupposition* that man was only a material being.

Empiricism almost completely stifled all attempts to explore man's spiritual or nonmaterial nature.

About this time in the nineteenth century another factor entered the field of knowledge; in 1859 Darwin's *Origin of Species* was published. The theory that man evolved from lower primates virtually exploded into the scientific arena. If empiricism reduced man to that which is physical, then evolution further impoverished man by demoting him to an animal.

Now two mighty forces were at work: *empiricism* (or "science" as it is generally known, teaching that man can be totally explained by that which is physical and measurable) and *evolution* (which said yes to empiricism and also insisted that man can further be understood by that which is animal).

One year after Darwin's *Origin of Species*; Gustav Fechner published *Elements of Psychophysics* (1860) in an attempt to mathematically specify the relationship between physical and mental events in man. The title of the book was derived from *psuche*, Greek for soul (that which makes up the nonmaterial nature of man), and physics, which is the science of motion, energy, and matter.

Now the stage was set for the appearance of psychology in the field of knowledge. The first psychological laboratory was founded by Wilhelm Wundt in 1879. Although he believed that man's soul and body were two different universes, the presuppositions that were to determine the eventual pursuit of this study were already established by 1) empiricism, 2) philosophy, and 3) evolution.

Although psychology is a new field of research as compared to philosphy, it has become an exceedingly broad arena, with many specialties. Emphases have been centered in social, educational, industrial, adolescent, physiological, and a host of other areas, including child psychology, animal psychology, comparative psychology, dynamic psychology, and functional psychology. This does not necessarily represent disunity in the field any more than surgery, internal medicine, othmology, or gynecology represent conflicts in the medical arena. We are talking about *specialization.*

There *are* areas of psychology, however, where there is much conflict. One of them is called "clinical psychology." This is the segment that attempts to solve personal difficulties, such as mental, emotional, and interpersonal dysfunctions.

More generally it is called the field of mental health. Emphases in this application include Gestaltism, Reality Therapy, Rational Emotive Therapy, Transactional Analysis, Psychoanalysis and Psychotherapy, with directive and non-directive variations in methodology. Authors like Freud, Jung, James, Horney, Sullivan, Adler, Glasser, Ellis, Rogers, Skinner, Maslow, and Mowrer have some sharply conflicting opinions in their books. These disagreements are often antithetical, so much so that if some are right, the others must be wrong.

All of the psychological emphases mentioned so far have at least one fatal flaw common to each of them: They do not include the personal God of the Bible in their doctrine. This is typical of all humanistic psychology.

To ignore God in the pursuit of knowledge is to become involved in futile speculations, to bring darkness instead of illumination into one's heart, and to become a fool instead of becoming wise. That is the risk all people take who leave God out of their knowledge.

Romans 1:21,22, in *The Christian Counselor's New Testament* (a new translation by J.E. Adams, Ph.D., published by Baker House) makes this quite clear:

> . . . because although people knew God, they didn't glorify Him as God or thank Him. Instead they became involved in futile speculations and their senseless hearts were darkened. Claiming that they were wise, they become fools.

This is not to say that all *psychologists* leave God out of their total area of knowledge. Some of them are God-fearing Christians who hold the Bible to be God's Word to man.

What is intended by the foregoing is to point out that the overall science itself, in its foundational presuppositions, in its world views, and in its body of information, ignore God.

Some scholars protest any attempt to bring God into every pursuit of knowledge, as though He would be an intruder who would thrust inaccurate data into the discipline being developed. This is being extremely shortsighted, for God's Word says:

> Lean on, trust and be confident in the Lord with all your heart and mind, and do not rely on your own sight or understanding. In all your ways know, recognize and acknowledge Him, and He will direct and make straight and plain your paths (Proverbs 3:5,6 Amplified Bible).

There is no greater source of help available to man than that which God offers to give to all those who seek it from Him. The advice David gave to his son, Solomon, is valid for all mankind:

> If you seek Him, He will let you find Him; but if you forsake Him, He will reject you forever. (1 Chronicles 28:9).

Solomon took his father's counsel, at least initially, and became known as the wisest man who ever lived. It was he who wrote the admonition quoted above from Proverbs.

It would be extremely difficult, if not actually impossible, to examine all the various emphases in psychology in a way that would show all the areas that are hostile to the Bible, to Christianity, and ultimately to God Himself. But the following classification of psychology used by Dr. Mark Cosgrove of Taylor University makes it possible to get a closer look at this problem.

Dr. Cosgrove in his book *The Essence of Human Nature* (Zondervan) and in a manuscript for his book *Psychology Gone Awry*, (Zondervan) classifies psychology under four headings which he calls "four forces in psychology": Behaviorism, Psycho-Analysis, Humanism, and Transpersonal Psychology. Psychology.

I understand him to say by this that behaviorism is the first force in that is the strongest, and the others come in the order of influence as indicated.

To clarify what I propose to do now, I have arranged these four forces in chart-like form showing the roots or intellectual soil from which they have developed:

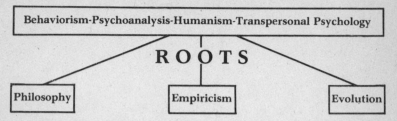

In the next sections each of these schools will be examined, but only to the extent that distinguishing features of each may be readily recognizable by nonprofessionals.

The goal is to show where these distinguishing features are in conflict with the Bible, and in doing so to show biblical alternatives that are available to all who love the truth in sincerity.

7

Behaviorism and Psychology

First let's look at Behaviorism as a definite school of psychological thought and practice.

The initial experiments in Wilhelm Wundt's (1882-1920) laboratory did not satisfy the empirical methods of science. To him, as was stated in the last chapter, the soul (or mind) and the human body were two separate universes. This dualism was part and parcel of the philosophy of Plato and many other Greek philosophers before and after him. It is and always has been a Bible doctrine too. It is warp and woof of the Old Testament as well as fundamental to the New.

Of course, the Bible version of the dualism in man is radically different from that of the Greek philosophers. But this difference is not the subject at this point. The subject is that dualism as a belief predates anything known formally as psychology. Whether Wundt (pronounced VOONT), got his idea from Greek philosophy or the Bible is a moot point, but for the purpose of this presentation it is only important to know that he believed in a dualistic nature of man. He believed in conscious mental experience but thought that all mental activity was the result of a function of the material, physical part of man—i.e., his brain. His research was designed to find how body and mind related to each other. Other questions in his studies were: How does the knower know the world around him? How does he communicate with other minds? What is the relation of conscious experience to reality?

What Wilhelm Wundt was doing in Germany, William James began doing in the United States. G. Stanley Hall, a student of both, started research in Johns Hopkins University in 1883. But neither did their methodology fit the empirical standards of investigation, because mental processes are not open to investigation by the empirical system.

John Watson (1878-1958), and American physiologist who is known as the father of behaviorism, insisted that psychology would best be studied by pure scientific (i.e., empirical) methods. He is quoted by Dr. Mark Cosgrove in *Psychology Gone Awry* (Zondervan) as saying:

> In 1912 the behaviorists reached the conclusion that they could no longer be content to work with intangibles and unapproachables. They decided either to give up psychology or to make it a natural science. . . . The behaviorist asks: Why don't we make what we can observe the real field of psychology? . . . Now what can be observed? Well, we can observe behavior—what the organism does or says.

So what started out to be a study of the dualism of man (his nonmaterial nature and his material nature) became a one-dimensional study.

At this point psychology took a wrenching departure from a true biblical position. There is much data to support the theme that man is more than a physical being, but the pure behavioristic psychologist, who is an empiricist, denies that spiritual dimension and insists that man is a machine or an animal or a combination of both, and that he has no mind or will but is totally preprogrammed by his genes or reprogrammed by his environment. Knowledge learned from studying animal behavior is interpolated or interposed into known facts about man, and the results are taken to prove that man is merely a highly intelligent animal that acts and reacts like a machine.

Behavioristic psychology completely ignores the biblical teaching that man is a created being made in the likeness and image of God (Genesis 1:26,27; 5:1; 9:6, James 3:9). It denies that man has a mind or a soul, which contradicts the plainest of Bible teaching. (See Matthew 10:28; 1 Thessalonians 5:23; Romans 12:1; Hebrews 4:12, to name only a few references.)

Behaviorism says that man has no ability to make a choice, but is wholly controlled by his environment. But the Bible says, *"Choose* ye this day whom ye will serve" (Joshua 24:15.) (See also Deuteronomy 30:19; Isaiah 7:15,16; Hebrews 11:25; Proverbs 22:1; Isaiah 66:3; Luke 10:42; Corinthians 8:19.) There are many more verses which prove not only that man can choose, but which teach that God insists that man make choices. Furthermore, He holds man responsible to make the *right* choices.

Behaviorism says that man is a prisoner of his environment, is locked into the machine-like universe in which he lives, and is himself part of that machine, trapped and programmed by it. Behaviorism says that man can be controlled by manipulating his environment. By a reward-and-punishment system, by good or bad primary and secondary reinforcements (which give either pleasure or pain), man can be made to be or do whatever the manipulator wishes.

Who it is that manipulates the manipulator is a question that is hard to answer. But an answer is necessary. If he too is controlled by his environment and is without power to choose and exercise his will, then the whole system is controlled by blind chance and impersonal fate. Therefore there would be no meaning or purpose in life for anyone. If the manipulator can choose and exercise his will, then the whole system is false and falls to the ground.

Skinner himself, the most important man in behaviorism, perhaps unwittingly but nonetheless forcefully reveals a flaw in his own doctrine. In Francis Schaeffer's book *Back to Freedom and Dignity* (pages 38, 39) is a quote from B.B.C.'s *The Listener* (September 30, 1971). Skinner says:

> . . . we must hope that a culture will emerge in which those who have power will use it for the general good. . . . If the

> power of a technology does indeed fall into the hands of despots, it will be because it has been rejected by men and women of good will.

In this slip-of-the-tongue statement Skinner reveals that he believes that men of good will have the power to choose or to reject.

Skinner is also quoted by Schaeffer in this same place as saying, "he accepts the control of those who pay him." By this Skinner implies that he rejects the control of those who do not pay him. Therefore he admits that he has power to choose. Thus Skinner finds it impossible to personally live within the framework of his own doctrine.

However, all that behaviorists teach is not false—men *are* influenced by their environment. Reward and pain *do* affect how a person acts. Man *does* have some elements in common with animals. Both he and they have feet, flesh, blood, hair, hearts, lungs, eyes, mouths.

But man, like his Creator, can transcend his environment. He need not be crushed by it. We all know of people who, against what seemed to be hopeless odds, rose above the squalor and poverty of ghettos to become scientists, doctors, judges, or champion athletes.

Behavior is indeed *influenced* by environment, but it is not necessarily *totally controlled* by it.

The study of animals can reveal much about man's physical being, but it sheds no light on how a man can think, speak, love, or understand concepts. From animals we can learn some things about man's physiology and biology, but can learn nothing about man's capacity to worship, to believe, to have faith, or about his ability to create, to write poems essays, to make and use tools. Neither his potential good nor his potential evil can be explained by observing animals.

Behaviorism is also correct in saying that man, as a material being, needs material things. Indeed, he needs material food for his material body. He also needs material clothing and houses to shelter his physical being. Other material things make life easier and more pleasant—i.e., cars, planes, trains, television, radio, tools, money, highways, and on and on.

But behaviorism cannot satisfactorily explain why man needs nonmaterial values even more than he needs material things—why he needs love, joy, peace, honesty, truth, justice, loyalty, friendship, equality, a sense of belonging, and other nonmaterial values. These things are not open to empirical investigation, according to the behaviorists, but they are very real and important to man. Man may have material things in superabundance, but he will find life unbearable if he is not also rich in nonmaterial, spiritual values. If he loves no one and no one loves him, and if he has no friends, no peace, no joy, no justice, he will be a candidate for deep depression and eventual suicide. The basis for this evaluation is that God designed man so that his life does not consist only of an abundance of things (Luke 12:15). Man certainly does need things. But he also needs to be rich in spiritual values because he is a spiritual creature.

Thus Behavioristic Psychology falls far short of giving satisfactory answers to what man really is and what he really needs.

Nothing but turning to God and His Word will give wholly adequate information about who and what man really is. Until man is recognized as having been created in God's likeness and image, no one will understand his real potential greatness. Until it is understood that man rebelled against his Creator and was badly damaged and flawed as a result, no one will ever understand the depth of his potential wickedness.

Furthermore, there is neither philosophy nor psychology that will enable man to solve all his personal and interpersonal problems, for the simple reason that these difficulties are generally the result of sin. Only the gospel of Jesus Christ can successfully offer the solution for problems developed in this way.

The behaviorists deal with bad behavior in three basic ways. First, they use the reward-punishment system (mentioned above). They try to manipulate the environment so that bad behavior brings a pleasant reward. This is supposed to create new habit patterns for the betterment of the persons involved.

A second method is through altering brain states by electric stimulation. In this method electrodes are implanted in specific areas of the brain that are known, for example, to encourage or to discourage aggression. This is a complicated, delicate procedure, but these implants have been used many times to control sexual behavior, appetite for food, and criminal tendencies, or to calm highly excitable persons or excite phlegmatic, passive individuals.

Brain surgery has been employed thousands of times to radically modify behavior that is undesirable. In this system, nerves leading to or from specific areas have been severed or sections of the brain have been removed. However, the results are so final and tenuous that social pressures have discouraged the procedure.

The rise of information about mood-altering drugs has made such radical surgery unnecessary. The development and application of drugs to alter human behavior is now widely used to control and modify a person's state of being. But too often this procedure leads to dependency and addiction, which pose worse problems than the ones for which treatment was originally given.

For detailed information on behavioristic psychology, I recommend Dr. Mark Cosgrove's *The Essence of Human Nature* and *Psychology Gone Awry* (Zondervan). It will be difficult to accept behaviorism as a valid discipline after reading these two books.

The Bible has a radically different method by which human behavior can be modified. Failure to follow this system is the biblical explanation for bad behavior. Faithful cooperation with the Bible method to correct and improve behavior is the way by which mankind can achieve conduct that benefits everyone. It is a system of commandments—things to do and things not to do. It consists of putting off bad habits and patterns and putting on proper behavior habits and patterns.

Details of this whole system are thoroughly described in the Bible. See Jay Adam's *the Christian Counselor's Manual* (Baker House), Chapters 17-19, for a detailed discussion of this theme.

A thorough description of this ethic involves the whole Christian message. A whole manuscript is needed to cover the theme. Only a few highlights will be given here. These include the following principles:

1)   Man is created in God's likeness and image but has rebelled against his Creator, a factual problem called *sin*. All people have sinned and come short of the glory of God (Romans 3:23).

2)   God has a plan to pardon man for his sin and to cleanse him from all the difficulties that his sin has caused. This is the message of the gospel of Jesus Christ (John 3:16).

3)   After man has accepted God's pardon, a design for life-changing growth is initiated. Old habits are to be replaced with new ones. New standards of conduct are established.

4)   The results are not always dramatic. Progress is often slow, gained bit-by-bit, a step at a time, but they are guaranteed by God's Word to all who cooperate with this knowledge. God also, through His Son, gives the Holy Spirit to strengthen, enable, and guide man through these processes.

5)   A man's behavior is in this way properly modified. Furthermore, victorious living becomes a reality to *all* who receive, believe, and obey this ethic.

This biblical process is totally antithetic to behavioristic psychology, and they will never be reconciled. It is impossible for any man to harmonize these extremes. To do so would ruin one or the other for the person who would dare try to do it.

8

Psychoanalysis and Psychology

Psychoanalysis is ordinarily attributed to Sigmund Freud, but he did not discover the theory alone. In 1880-82 a Viennese physician, Josef Bruer, while working with a woman who was the victim of severe hysteria, discovered that this was a method by which she subconsciously escaped facing unpleasant memories experienced while caring for her very sick father when she was a child. Apparently she had been frightened and overwhelmed by something related to this. Facing the problem was too much for her. Lengthy study revealed that she frequently became hysterical to escape memories of the painful ordeal. This had become a way of life to her. These data were learned from the lady while she was under hypnosis. When she was shown the source of her hysteria she recovered completely.

Later Dr. Bruer collaborated with Sigmund Freud, and in 1895 they published a book which described Bruer's discoveries and therapy. Freud extended the studies and developed a theory of diagnosis and treatment, which he called psychoanalysis.

The theory says man has a mental apparatus composed of the *id,* which is a reservoir of man's instinctive impulses; the *ego*, or self, which is part of man's mind that is modified by the influences of the world around him, and the *super-ego*, which develops in the id and dominates the ego. In this triad man is subjected to all sorts of inhibitions, conflicts, and stresses because his ego is oversocialized by the world around him, by society, by his church, and, in particular, by his parents. (This later problem Freud called The Oedepus Complex.) This conflict between the id and the ego is heightened by the super-ego, which acts to seek conformity of the ego to parental, social, and moral standards. Thus the victim is forced into conduct and/or attitudes that cause great problems of inner turmoil. Therefore, conditions that are called mental illness develop, which produce problems like depression, psychosis and schizophrenia (to name a few). Psychoanalysis is then in order, so they say.

Sexual instincts and ego-education are sources of great conflict, according to the psychoanalysis philosophy. This becomes a pandora's box of concern for both the counselor and counselee. Deep problems with guilt are faced. The counselor tries to eliminate the guilt by claiming to be false.

Thus there are three areas that receive much attention in this kind of therapy: 1) *society,* including especially the church, for it (according to Freud) most severely inhibits man's ego; 2) *the family* (both parents and grandparents), for they also build barriers in their children's egos; and 3) *sexual drives* that demand free expression (so says Freud) but are suppressed by society (especially the church) and the family.

By a system of transference, the counselee develops emotional relationships with the therapist. Both affectionate and hostile relationships develop. However, these are not necessarily based on reality. This hostility or affection is transferred in fantasy from parents, society, or the church to the counselor. This is looked on as an opportunity for the therapist to reeducate the counselee and correct the inhibiting influences of his childhood by destroying the validity of moral training of both the church and the family.

In 1909, G. Stanley Hall (mentioned in the last chapter) invited Freud and C.G. Jung to lecture on psychoanalysis in the U.S. The whole thing was met with hostility. Perhaps this was chiefly because of the extreme emphasis laid on sexuality, a concept for which our society was not yet prepared. But the violent resistance merely spread fuel on the psychological fires then being ignited. Psychoanalysis was here to stay.

Initially opposed by the medical profession, it later became a branch of medicine when psychiatry adopted it as a valid therapy. After World War Two there was a steady growth of psychoanalysis both in the field of medicine (psychiatry) and in psychology.

It rapidly became the strongest force in psychology. But it was seriously challenged by psychologists who called themselves behaviorists.

Now it is relegated to second place. Meanwhile the behaviorists have developed into the leading force in psychology.

It seems to this writer that psychoanalysis cannot possibly survive, because as a therapy it has three serious drawbacks: 1) It is lengthy (often years are involved); 2) it is expensive (the cost of such treatment is so high that only the rich can afford it. The poor must accept it from welfare organizations or other charity); 3) the probability of successful results is so slight that hope is seldom held forth to a counselee. Nevertheless, it has millions of adherents who know of no other place to go. Thus there exists a vast mission field for biblical counseling procedures.

Another factor in its diminishing influence (besides the challenge of other psychologies like behaviorism, humanism, and transpersonal psychology) is the fact that it is being attacked by knowledgeable men. Martin L. Gross's book *The Psychological Society* is severely critical of psychotherapy. Christine Russell, *Washington Star* staff writer (in the *Washington Star*, Thursday, May 4, 1978), quotes Martin Gross as saying, "all psychotherapy is false." Out of a question-and-answer interview the following is written:

Q. You mean the profession is worried as to whether or not they are helping people?

A. Exactly. You know why? There are a lot of honest men

in the profession. They are honest. They are not competent because there is nothing to be competent about. But they are honest and people who want to help. A committee was appointed by the American Psychiatric Association, headed by Dr. Robert Spitzer of Columbia Presbyterian Medical School, to revise the diagnostic manual. They have decided the following: The word neurosis has no meaningful psychiatric definition. As of 1979 the word neurosis is out of psychiatry. For 50 years we've been told we're neurotic, now it no longer exists. It's being replaced with a simple word: anxiety. Anxiety we understand. Rollo May said that anxiety is what separates us from animals and a goal for improvement, for intellect, a goal for religion. Now, not only is the word neurosis being thrown out of the manual, but all psychological definitions and all Freudian definitions, and it will read like a medical manual.

Q. Has this manual been accepted?

A. It has been accepted by the executive committee. The Freudians, the psychoanalysts, the psychotherapists are up in arms and there is nothing they can do about it.

Q. Why are you particularly critical of psychoanalysis and Freudian theories?

A. All of psychotherapy is false. There is no expert knowledge of the human mind—none. Any expert knowledge of the human mind exists only by intuition and only among people who have the talent for healing. Talent might be a schoolteacher, a cabdriver, a policeman or perhaps even a psychiatrist. A psychiatrist can be a healer by accident, but not because he is a psychiatrist. There is nothing he can learn that can teach him to heal. The reason is healing by talking is faith healing. Navajo witch doctors do it, African witch doctors do it, students can do it, anybody who has the talent. It's nothing you can learn. You can't be trained for it. It's a talent. It's a talent that a small percentage of the profession has. It's not that I am against Freudian theories more than others, it's just that Freudian theories are pure nonsense. It's the distilled nonsense of Sigmund Freud which has been watered down and become a little more common-sensical as it goes further out from Freud. But it's always, in total, non-knowledge. We know it's non-knowledge because [being on] the waiting list will do as well, placebos do as well, amateurs do as well.

There are other writers speaking out too. Dr. Thomas A. Szasz, a psychiatrist and author of *Myth of Mental Illness* (Harper and Row) places the "disease" treated by psychoanalysis in the realm of mythology. Dr. Jay Adams in his books *The Big Umbrella* and *Competent to Counsel* argues devastatingly to refute the validity of this therapy. These three books alone have done much to undermine Freud's total approach to psychology.

There are several ways to determine whether a psychology is rooted in Freudianism.

1) If it looks into an adult's childhood and his parent-child relationship, it is probably Freudian.

2) If it blames society (especially the church), it quite likely is Freudian.

3) If it blames sexual inhibition, it is almost certain to be Freudian.

4) If it searches and explores the subconscious mind for answers, it certainly comes from that source.

5) If it uses any of the foregoing to relieve the counselee of any sense of guilt or responsibility, its roots are definitely in Sigmund Freud's school of psychoanalytic thought.

While it is true that our parent's sins do influence us—

Exodus 20:5—
Thou shalt not bow down thyself to them, nor serve them: for I the Lord thy God am a jealous God, visiting the iniquity of the fathers upon the children unto the third and fourth generation of them that hate me.

Exodus 23:7—
Keeping mercy for thousands, forgiving iniquity and transgression and sin, and that will by no means clear the guilty; visiting the iniquity of the fathers upon the children, and upon the children's children, unto the third and to the fourth generation.

Numbers 14:18—
The Lord is longsuffering, and of great mercy, forgiving iniquity and transgression, and by no means clearing the guilty, visiting the iniquity of the fathers upon the children unto the third and fourth generation.

Deuteronomy 5:9—
Thou shalt not bow down thyself unto them, nor serve them, for I the Lord thy God am a jealous God, visiting the iniquity of the fathers upon the children unto the third and fourth generation of them that hate me.

It is also true that each person is fully responsible before God for how he reacts to the sins of other people, even his parents' sins. Each person will answer for his *own* sins, no matter who influenced him to commit violations of God's law.

Ezekiel 3:20—
When a righteous man doth turn from his righteous-

ness, and commit iniquity, and I lay a stumblingblock before him, he shall die; because thou has not given him warning, he shall die in his sin, and his righteousness which he hath done shall not be remembered; but his blood will I require at thine hand.

Ezekiel 18:4—
Behold, all souls are mine; as the soul of the father, so also the soul of the son is mine; the soul that sinneth, it shall die.

No one can use another person's behavior as an excuse for his own actions to escape either the responsibility for or the consequences of his own sins.

It is true that society and its pressures influence us. But these pressures do not have to control or determine our lives. We can live above these pressures. We can do what Phillips so eloquently suggests in his paraphrase of Romans 12:2: "Don't let the world squeeze you into its own mold, but let God remold your minds from within."

As Christians we are *in* the society of the world but we are not *of* it. We do not have to helplessly conform to it. We can overcome it.

John 13:1—
Now before the feast of the passover, when Jesus knew that his hour was come that he should depart out of this world unto the Father, having loved his own which were in the world, he loved them unto the end.

John 17:14,15—
I have given them thy word; and the world hath hated them because they are not of the world, even as I am not of the world. I pray not that thou shouldest take them out of the world, but that thou shouldest keep them from the evil.

> **1 John 5:4,5—**
> For whatsoever is born of God over cometh the world; and this is the victory that overcometh the world, even our faith. Who is he that overcometh the world, but he that believeth that Jesus is the Son of God?

The emphasis of psychoanalysis on the subconscious levels of the mind may not be entirely wrong. Actually it may shed some light on what the Bible calls the heart, out of which are the issues of life. If there is a similarity, then what Freud taught about it can be refuted totally by the Bible.

One final word about psychoanalysis—it is not to be taken lightly. It is still here; its demise, although quite possible, is not just around the corner. All students of psychology and counseling will run into it quite often. Sometimes it lurks behind what seems to be, on the surface, gospel truth. But it never is. Its roots are deeply embedded in the soil of secularistic humanism and godless evolution. Freud called himself "a godless Jew" and was hostile to the Bible and Christianity. He believed that his father had been severely humiliated by Christians. Some think Freud was motivated by this to use his skills and knowledge in ways that would avenge his father's embarrassment. Others think that the fact Freud opened his business on an Easter Sunday was done in contempt for that Christian memorial of Christ's resurrection.

While some psychoanalysis may make it easier to understand a scriptural principle we must never let ourselves syncretize psychoanalysis and the Bible. God Himself will oppose that.

9

Humanism and Psychology

To many psychologists, behaviorism has so dehumanized man that he has ceased to exist as man. In other words, to the pure behaviorist, man exists as a machine or as an animal; he does not have qualities and traits that differentiate him from an animal or a machine. Stripping man of his dignity as a human and demoting him to the status of an animal or a machine is a good thing, according to them, for this forces man to face truth, so they say, and takes him out of a world of fantasy and places him squarely into the real world and the real facts about himself.

Psychoanalysis also tends to dehumanize man, for it portrays him as helplessly trapped by inner, subconscious forces beyond his control and as being dependent upon an elite segment of society i.e., psychiatrists and/or psychologists who are psychoanalysists) to direct him out of his dilemma.

These two psychologies failed to answer questions about man that many psychologists were asking. Does man have no more dignity than an animal or freedom than a machine? Is he helplessly programmed, predetermined by blind fate? Is he a prisoner of the mechanical universe in which he lives? Or is he a free, moral agent, able to be self-determined and capable of solving his own problems? Is he able to transcend the forces around him? The search for these answers (and others) led to another school of psychological thought that has become known as the Third Force in psychology or, as it is popularly called, "Humanistic Psychology" or "Human Potential Psychology."

The label "humanism" is given to it because it aggrandizes and champions human beings (quite unlike behaviorism and psychoanalysis, which degrade humanity). To the humanist, man has dignity and worth. He also has the ability and wisdom to solve all his problems without the advice or direct instruction of another human. All man needs, according to the humanistic psychologist, is the opportunity to see his problem and his potential. Then he by himself can solve his problem and reach his potential.

To this school of thought man is inherently good as well as wise and capable. Given opportunity, this goodness will be displayed along with his wisdom and capabilities.

Dr. Mark Cosgrove in *Psychology Gone Awry* quotes Carl Rogers as saying that man ". . . is a person who creates meaning in life, a person who embodies a dimension of subjective freedom. He is a figure who, though he may be alone in a vastly complex universe, and though he may be part and parcel of that universe and its destiny, is also able in his inner life to transcend the material universe."

Cosgrove also writes, "In general, humanistic psychology sees man's healthy, conscious self as the subject matter of psychology. The data of concern in this field are. . . .

> Those human capacities and potentialities that have little or no place, either in positive or behaviorist theory or in classical psychoanalytic theory: e.g., love, creativity, self, growth, organism, basic need for gratification, self actualization, higher values, being, becoming, spontaneity, play, humor, affection, naturalness, warmth, ego transcendence, objectivity, autonomy, responsibility, meaning, fair play, transcendental experience, psychological health, and related concepts."

The above quotation is from the American Association for Humanistic Psychology Progress Report, J.F.T. Bugental, "The Third Force" *Journal of Humanistic Psychology 4* (1) 1964, page 22. Note that Dr. Bugental says that the data studied by humanistic psychology have little or no place in behaviorism or psychoanalysis.

A little reflection on their data in contrast to what the behaviorists and psychoanalysts have to say about man clearly portrays the difference in their emphasis and those of the humanist. In contrast to behaviorism, humanism sees man as two-dimensional; i.e., he has a nonmaterial as well as a material nature. It also believes that he has unlimited potential for good and that he has great value, and that his basic motivation is for good and he has little, if any, intrinsic instincts for evil.

This brand of psychology also resists Freud's theory that man's inner drives are centered in physical satisfaction and aggression. They also reject Skinner's theory that man's nature is so sufficiently passive that it can be molded toward good or evil depending upon the contingencies of reinforcement in his environment.

Instead, humanists believe that man's inner drives are aimed at self-improvement and that he naturally tends to resist the bad influences of his environment; if he can fully realize his potential, he will transcend all that rips him up and tears him down and eventually builds himself into the wonderful being he really is. Thus he is the "Captain of his fate, the Master of his Soul."

This belief is one of the reasons that humanistic psychology insists on the value of *strong self-love* and *a good self-image*. Biblical alternatives to these selfisms are discussed in Chapters 10 and 11.

With all this potential in man, the humanist psychologist is hard-pressed to show examples of it ever having been achieved by anyone. Most of them freely admit that few indeed, if any, have ever risen to this potential.

In fact, almost all the disciplines of higher learning are aware that there is something wrong in man. They all realize that he is not what he can be, but they try to explain this flaw as follows:

Behaviorism says man's nature and his environment is the problem.

Philosophy says the flaw is in man's irrational thinking.
Sociology calls it his cultural lag.
History defines it as part of the class struggle.
Humanism calls it human weakness and ignorance.
Biology says it is a primitive instinct left over from evolution.
Shakespeare names it the tragic flaw.
The Bible calls it *Sin*.
Adapted from a taped lecture by Mark Cosgrove
(Probe Ministries—Christian Free University).

Humanistic psychologists have several possible explanations for this malfunction in human beings. They say it is because 1) man is ignorant of or 2) blind to his potential; 3) man simply fails to use his inner resources; 4) he has poor habit patterns; 5) he has poor education; 6) he is a victim of Western culture that teaches man to fear his instincts; 7) he has a lack of courage to reach for his highest potential; or 8) he is lulled to complacency by a desire to maintain the status quo.

This branch of psychology is suffering from the same fatal error mentioned previously: It has left God out of its knowledge and as a result has wandered far from absolute truth.

However, humanistic psychology is nevertheless closer to God's truth than either behaviorism or psychoanalysis.

First, man is indeed a great being, as they say. But he has much greater potential than humanism allows. Man is created in God's likeness and image and, as a Christian, is predestinated to be conformed to the likeness of the resurrected Jesus Christ; i.e., he can be restored completely to what he was created to be. God has a plan for this transformation.

Man, unaided by God, cannot even imagine what he is capable of becoming, according to 1 Corinthians 2:9 (NIV)—

No eye has seen,
No ear has heard,
No man has conceived
What God has prepared
For those who love Him.

Therefore, no mere man has a complete idea of how great his potential really is. It can only be known to man by special revelation from God. It can only be achieved by following God's instructions and doing so by His help. Man's attempts to identify his true potential and his attempt to reach it apart from God's assistance are totally futile. So humanism, in rejecting God, bars itself from the absolute truth it tries to proclaim.

Humanism is more readily accepted than behaviorism because it appeals to man's selfish desires. It is less obtrusive than behaviorism in its nonbiblical position and therefore more easily invades true Christian beliefs. Unfortunately, much of its error is already syncretized into Christianity. The teaching that self-love and self-image are virtues worthy to be pursued is far more humanistic than biblical, as will be shown later.

Another error of humanistic psychology that has been taken into Christianity is *nondirective counseling methodology.* The counselor with pure Rogerian emphasis, seldom, if ever, gives advice or identifies problems directly. Rather, by reflecting back *to* the counselee information given *by* the counselee the counselor tries to get his client to "see things as they are for himself." Greatly oversimplified, it goes something like this:

Counselee: I have a real serious problem at home.

Counselor: Oh? Do I understand you correctly? You have a domestic difficulty?

Counselee: Exactly. My wife and I are always fighting.

Counselor: Hmmm. So you have a marital difficulty?

Counselee: Yeah! I don't know what I'm going to do but I gotta do something—quick.

Counselor: I see you are bewildered. Maybe a little anxious? And you feel time is running out?

Counselee: You're exactly right, Doctor. I'm worried sick. What shall I do?

Counselor: You're worried and you want to know what to do, aren't you? Tell me your *true feelings** about this.

And on and on the session goes. The counselor is always care-

---

*Feelings are the important factors in Rogerian counseling.

ful to avoid giving advice, for that would imply that the counselee isn't able to see his problem or the answer. This would deny a basic tenent of humanism—i.e., that man is able to solve his own problems, and only needs to identify them on his own. Therefore, the counselor, by skillfully mirroring back to the counselee what he has to say, tries to get him to discover for himself what the real problem is. Then, according to the Rogerian system, he can also discover, by and for himself, the solution to his problem.

It is true that facts *discovered* by one's self are more readily remembered than facts *prescribed* from outside sources. And it is a worthy goal to strive for by any teacher. But to be totally nondirective in helping a student (or counselee) discover facts is a bit of naiveness difficult for a veteran teacher to accept. And it is even more difficult for a biblically oriented teacher to accept.

The Bible is highly directive. It pulls no punches. It is full of *"thou shalts"* and *"thou shalt nots."* It is loaded with commandments. It tells its adherents to rebuke, to exhort, to correct, to confront, to proclaim. It calls sin by its particular name. Illicit sex is not extramarital activity; it is adultery that brings a blot and stain to the participants. It is sin, and the Bible demands confession, repentance, restitution, and forgiveness. Like Nathan and David, a '"Thou-art-the-man" technique is in order (2 Samuel 12:1-14).

The biblical counselor is directive and gives information, identifies problems, discusses answers, warns of penalties, asks specific questions, gives specific answers, and insists on certain responses. He is biblical.

The nondirective counselor seldom, if ever, does any of the foregoing. He deals with feelings and attitudes which he interprets. To him, feelings (rather than behavior) are important. The intellectual content of what the counselee says is less important than what he feels about the content. This is because feelings and experiences are the principal parts of reality in humanistic psychology. Subjectivity is more important than objectivity. This counselor is not biblically oriented. He is humanistically oriented.

10

Humanism and Self-Love

Recently while lecturing in a California church, a lady who was a total stranger to me but well-known in the congregation asked a question.

"Can you give me a brief statement as to what you consider the most difficult problem I face as a Christian?"

I was seated on a high stool behind a small lecturn. I looked intently at my questioner. Then, sliding off the stool, I strode to a blackboard and chalked one six-inch-high word:

SELF

When I turned from the blackboard so all could see the word, there were gales of laughter. I did not see the joke. My upturned palms and bewildered expressions plead silently for an answer. More laughter.

"What did I do wrong?"

"You did nothing wrong," the questioner said. "You just wrote my name on the blackboard. I am Mrs. Self. That's my name."

Her friends thought it uproariously funny, but even in that lighthearted banter a real truth stood out. We are all our own worst enemy.

Only a few books outside the Bible point to this problem of self more forcefully than does Earl Jabay in his book *The Kingdom of Self*. He starts with "His Majesty the Baby," and traces the tyrannical self from infancy all the way to egocentric adulthood. It isn't a pretty picture. But all who read those chapters (II through IV) will wince more than once. I know I did.

A blanket endorsement of Dr. Jabay's work is not intended, nor is this a hint of sly criticism. It is brought up simply to state that there is not much literature that better portrays selfism as it really is, warts and all.

Many books today champion two major selfisms as though they were high-priority goals to strive for: self-love and self-image. Many Christian writers support this view.

Some writers oppose this. Dr. Jay Adams does so quite effectively. He is a well-known, often-published author of many books on biblical counseling. His work is creating a counseling revolution in the church community. He thoroughly disagrees with this love-yourself theme. His opinions are worth careful reading as he refutes the flimsy foundation of this teaching.

The rest of this chapter will deal with self-love, and the next chapter will deal with the self-image theme.

At this point it is important to repeat that nothing in this entire work is directed against persons. Only *positions* are in question. The persons are, without exception, made in the image and likeness of God and are therefore to be highly regarded and respected. But this exalted status of all human beings does not guarantee that their positions conform to what God has to say.

If the Bible does in fact teach that we are to love ourselves and concern ourselves about a good self-image, then it is incumbent on all of us to obediently pursue and develop a good (?) self-love and self-image. But does the Bible teach this love-thyself theme? That is the question.

I do not think it does. Neither does John Piper, Assistant Professor of Biblical studies at Bethel College, in St. Paul, Minnesota. His article in *Christianity Today* entitled "Is Self-Love Biblical?" is a resounding rebuke of the theology that says it is biblical teaching. (See August 12, 1977 issue, page 6.)

Nor does John R. W. Stott, Rector Emeritus of All Souls Church in London, agree that the Bible teaches man to love himself. In an issue of *Christianity Today*, Stott agreed with Piper in casting a vote against self-loveism. These two articles should convince any reasonable, unbiased mind that self-love is not a biblical virtue.

I want to use the data given by these two Bible teachers to reinforce the biblical teaching about self-love. First, the commandment "Thou shalt love thy neighbor as thyself" appears at least eight times in the Bible: Leviticus 19:18; Matthew 19:19; 22:39; Mark 12:31; Luke 10:27; Romans 13:9; Galatians 5:14; and James 2:8.

There is no question about the fact that we are commanded to love our neighbors. The question is, Does the "as thyself" also constitute a command? Jesus did not think so. He said, "Thou shalt love the Lord thy God with all thy heart, and with all thy soul, and with all thy mind. This is the *FIRST* and greatest commandment. And the *SECOND* is like unto it: Thou shalt love thy neighbor as thyself. On these *TWO* commandments hang all the law and the prophets" (Matthew 22:37-40).

Most proponents of the "love-thyself" theory see three commandments here: love God, love your neighbor, and love yourself. Jesus saw only two. "On these TWO commandments hang all the law and the prophets," He said.

John Stott gives three reasons why the "as thyself" phrase cannot be construed to be a command. First, to do so is unacceptable grammatically. The command is not to love both thy neighbor and thyself. Instead, it is an injunction to love your neighbor as you do in fact love yourself. The Bible never teaches or encourages self-love; it merely acknowledges that man does indeed love himself. Paul recognized this and wrote in Ephesians 5:29, "No man ever yet hated his flesh." It would not change the meaning of Matthew 22:39 if it read, "You shall love your neighbor as much as you do in fact love yourself." The "as thyself" is an adverbial phrase, not an imperative. It modifies the verb, love, describing the degree of the love one is to have for his neighbor. This Scripture is another way of expressing the Golden Rule: "Do unto others as you would have them do unto you."

So grammatically speaking, it is easy to refute the idea that we are *commanded* to love ourselves.

But that still leaves the question, Does "as thyself" *encourage* one to love himself even though he is not commanded to do so? Again the answer is negative, for it fails linguistically.

The Greek verb *love* in these verses is *agapao*. The word always carries in its definition the element of sacrifice and service to others. It is one of the richest expressions in Greek when it reveals one's attitude toward God and to a neighbor. Paul describes its components in 1 Corinthians 13, one of the Bible's most eloquent chapters.

But how are we going to sacrifice ourselves to serve ourselves? Self-sacrifice is a virtue when applied to other people, but self-serving is ugly. It is selfishness and it is sinful. Stott, writing about having agape for one's self, states, "The concept is non-sensical. Agape love cannot be self-directed; for if it is, it destroys itself. It ceases to be self-sacrifice and becomes self-service." The concept, therefore, dies linguistically.

Furthermore, the self-love theory is unacceptable theologically, for it makes the Bible recommend a practice in one place, only to object to it in another. Place the self-love concept parallel to 2 Timothy 3:1-5 and you will see a serious conflict.

Matthew 22:39	2 Timothy 3:1-5
. . . Thou shalt love thy neighbor as thyself.	This know also, that in the last days perilous times shall come. For men shall be lovers of their own selves, covetous, boasters, proud, blasphemers, disobedient to parents, unthankful, unholy, without natural affection, truce-breakers, false accusers, incontinent, fierce, despisers of those that are good, traitors, heady, high-minded, lovers of pleasures more than lovers of God; having a form of godliness, but denying the power thereof; from such turn away.

If Matthew 22:39 teaches us to love ourselves, we have a conflict with Timothy. Then compare it to Mark 8:34,35 and Luke 9:23 and observe a second contradiction.

Matthew 22:39

Mark 8:34,35

And when he had called the people unto him with his disciples also, he said unto them, Whosoever will come after me, let him deny himself, and take up his cross, and follow me. For whosoever will save his life shall lose it; but whosoever shall lose his life for my sake and the gospel's, the same shall save it."

. . . Thou shalt love thy neighbor as thyself.

Luke 9:23

And he said to them all, if any man will come after me, let him deny himself, and take up his cross daily, and follow me.

The conflict is an obvious theological problem, for it makes the Bible contradict itself. The Greek word used here for "deny" is *aparneomai*. It means to deny utterly, to renounce, to reject utterly, to abstain from. The Amplified Bible says it means to "forget, ignore, disown—to lose sight of himself and his own interests." While this contradicts the self-love theory, it harmonizes with the exhortation in Mark 8:35 that encourages Christians to lose (i.e. give up) their lives for Christ's and the gospel's sake.

Self-love is not taught in the Bible. It comes right out of humanism and is an integral part of self-autonomy. It is not a virtue. It is a sin.

What shall we then say? Are we to hate ourselves? Denigrate ourselves? Not at all. Note what Dr. Stott says in his *Christianity Today* article:

We should be able to agree that self-depreciation is a false and damaging attitude. Those who regard a human being as nothing but a programmed machine (behaviorists) or an absurdity (existentialists) or a naked ape (humanistic evolutionists) are all denigrating our creation in God's image. True, we are also rebels against God and deserve nothing at his hand except judgment, but our fallenness has not entirely destroyed our God-likeness. More important still, in spite of our revolt against him, God has loved, redeemed, adopted, and re-created us in Christ. Anthony Hoekema is surely right, in his excellent little work, *The Christian Looks at Himself* (Eerdmans 1975), that 'the ultimate basis for our positive self-image must be God's acceptance of us in Christ,' (p. 102). If he has accepted us, should we not accept ourselves?

This self-acceptance is not self-love by any stretch of one's imagination.

To a true Christian, the opposite of self-love is not self-hatred or self-depreciation. The real believer does not swing to either extreme. He sees himself as God sees him—made in God's likeness and God's image. He is badly marred, scarred, and damaged by sin, but he is not beyond repair and recovery. He knows that God has accepted him as he is, and in His on way and at His own pace he is being restored, predestined to be conformed to the image of God's perfect Son, Jesus our Lord (Romans 8:29).

That believer is grateful to God. He appreciates what God has done and is doing for him. He loves God wholeheartedly —with all his mind, heart, and soul—because he realizes how much God loves him. John explains this in his First Epistle: "We love Him because He first loved us" (John 4:19).

Because this wonderful love of God is shed abroad in his heart, the redeemed sinner disregards himself and his own self-interests and instead dedicates himself to loving his neighbor. This truth is wonderfully shown in John Piper's "Is Self-Love Biblical." His text was:

And, behold, a certain lawyer stood up and tempted him, saying, "Master, what shall I do to inherit eternal life?" He said unto him, "What is written in the law? How readest thou?" And he answering said, "Thou shalt love the Lord thy God with all thy heart, and with all thy soul, and with all thy strength, and with all thy mind, and thy neighbor as thyself." And He said unto him, "Thou hast answered right: this do, and thou shalt live" (Luke 10:25-28).

Here we have a narrative about a misunderstanding of the command in Leviticus 19:18, "Thou shalt love thy neighbor as thyself." In it we see a man trying to embarrass Jesus with a question that appeared to be very spiritual and important: "What shall I do to inherit eternal life?" But the question was insincere, and so was the lawyer who asked it. He apparently wanted to force Jesus into a trap.

Always right to the point, Jesus cut straight through this man's duplicity. Instead of being on the spot, Jesus turned the tables, and the lawyer was in a position to be embarrassed.

"What shall I do to inherit eternal life?"

"What is written in the law? How do you read?"

"Thou shalt love the Lord thy God with all thy heart, and with all thy soul, and with all thy strength, and with all thy mind, and thy neighbor as thyself."

Now a paraphrase:

"You knew the answer—What's the *real* reason you ask it?"

Thus the lawyer was exposed as being insincere, and not a seeker after truth. That he was embarrassed is evident from Luke's analysis: "But he, willing to justify himself, said unto Jesus, And who is my neighbor?"

Jesus' answer touched lightly on "Who is the neighbor I'm supposed to love?" but gave a devastating reply on *how* a neighbor is to show love.

We all know the story. A man had fallen victim to highway bandits, was stripped of his clothing, and was left severely wounded on the dusty roadside. Both a priest and a Levite in turn saw the victim but refused involvement. They each passed by, leaving the battered victim exposed to the elements. No love was shown—none at all.

Then came a despised Samaritan and showed compassion. He demonstrated what it meant to love a neighbor. He interrupted the schedule of his journey. He took a calculated risk. How did he know this wasn't a booby trap, a plan designed to give hiding bandits access to another victim? The facts are that the Samaritan did not know. But he took a calculated risk. He gave assistance; he treated the wounds with his own wine and oil; he gave up his own transportation unit to ease the difficulty of getting the victim to a safe place for recovery. He spent the rest of the day and that night nursing and caring for the wounded man.

The next day he paid the injured man's bill out of his own money. He left extra funds and obligated himself to a possible future financial obligation. Then, about 24 hours late in his own business schedule, he left with a promise to return and finish any leftover tasks.

Who was this done for? A friend? A relative? An associate? No. It was done for a total stranger by a man whose only obligation to the victim was the unfortunate man's plight plus the command to love one's neighbor.

Jesus then asked a searching question on being a neighbor to someone in need: "Who was neighbor to him that fell among thieves?" Of course it was the Samaritan, who totally disregarded himself, interrupted his schedule, took calculated risks, used up his money, and accepted debt to help a stranger simply because he was in need.

Where is self-love taught here? Is it not possible that self-love, self-interest, and self-preservation prompted the Levite and the priest to keep out of range and pass by without stopping to help? Were they not prompted by self-interest motives? Isn't the Samaritan's conduct laudable? Does not the action of the other two seem shabby in comparison? This seems to denounce self-love, not recommend it.

John Piper writes a searching paragraph about this.

The point of Jesus' parable was to show that the lawyer's request for a definition of "neighbor" was simply skirting the real issue, namely, the kind of person he himself was. The lawyer's problem was not to define the word "neighbor". His problem—and the problem of every human being—was to become the kind of person who, because of compassion, cannot pass by on the other side. No truly compassionate or merciful heart can stand idly by while the mind examines a suffering candidate to see if he fits the definition of neighbor.

Was not Jesus telling the lawyer that he was the selfish Priest, the Levite, and not the good Samaritan? Does not the parable speak similarly to most of us, too?

Today's error on "Love thy neighbor as thyself" concerns a different issue. The error just discussed was *who* is my neighbor. The answer is, Don't look for a neighbor to love but be a neighbor to the needy. The current error is, "To love my neighbor I must first love myself." I have already shown this to be wrong because of grammatical, theological, and linguistical problems.

"Okay," you say. "If the Bible does not teach self-love as a desirable virtue, or a necessary one, where does the doctrine come from?"

Good question, and the answer is simple. It is the fruit of man's determination to be autonomous, to make his own standards. It is self on the throne of man's heart, crying, "Look at me. Am I not wonderful? Lovable?" It is part and parcel of Third-Force, Humanistic Psychology.

11

Humanism and Self-Image

In this chapter we face a bigger problem than in the previous chapter, for when writing about loving one's self there were at least a few Bible verses to work with, all of which were useful in proving that the doctrine of self-love is not taught in the Scriptures. The Scriptures acknowledge that man does indeed love himself, but they do not recommend the practice as a virtue.

But when studying the self-image theories there is no Scripture that mentions the subject by name. If the Bible were the only source of information available we would know very little about it. But when we look at this doctrine as taught by secular writers, we learn some startling things that seem to have roots in the Bible.

The principle of the self-image has been discovered by men like Maxwell Maltz, the great plastic surgeon who noted that new faces often transformed the total personalities of patients whose deformed features had been corrected by surgery. This he understood. But what about the patients who had ugly scars or facial deformities corrected but still felt ugly and unacceptable? Even when those transformations were dramatic, where beauty had replaced homeliness and ugly features were made classic by the surgeon's skills, some patients still believed themselves to be ugly, insisting that there was little or no change at all.

Dr. Maltz eventually concluded that every person has a

mental image of what he believes about himself. And unless the surgical changes in a patient's outerself are accompanied by a change for the better in the mental image he has in his innerself, the patient will not believe there has been satisfactory surgery. Neither compliments nor testimony from friends nor before-and-after photographs help these people see any improvement. The self-image held by them controls what they believe in spite of the outward physical changes.

In this manner the theory of self-image was developed as a key to personality changes. In brief it can be said accurately that the mental pictures one holds in his mind have more to do with his personality than the actual outer facts have on it. I don't know who originated the use of this theme, but many writers have adopted it. Many psychologists and psychiatrists use it.

Furthermore, the theme has spread beyond personality development and beyond self-acceptance problems, and has become a key to success in almost all areas of life. Salesmen, writers, athletes, actors, and preachers, to name a few, have found this theory a workable methodology for self-improvement. How-to books, taped lectures, films, and seminar speakers have flood our society with this message. The sheer volume of it, like Mount Everest, is overwhelming by its vastness. It seems to be taught everywhere—even in the Bible.

And it works! In varying degrees it actually does get amazing results. It is a powerful, formidable force for good or for evil. But like many powerful drugs, it also has potentially bad side effects even when used for good goals.

The pill designed to give more-positive birth control has made some women sterile. Thalidomide, developed to cure one problem, created a worse one. Many drugs are dangerous, even lethal, when the directions of the manufacturer or the prescribing doctor are not followed scrupulously.

So it is with the self-image doctrine. Unless mankind uses it according to his Creator's instructions, it will develop side effects that can destroy the purpose for which God designed it to be used. Yes, I believe it is part of God's plan for his creatures' good. But as used today it has a potential danger that must not be overlooked.

Consider the thought expressed in Proverbs 23:7: "as he thinketh in his heart, so is he." When it is realized that people think in pictures, or images, it can be seen that this verse does support the theory that a good self-image brings good results and a bad self-image brings bad results.

You can test, right now the theory that you think in terms of mental pictures or images. Think of the word "car." Your mind does not see the letter-combination C-A-R. It sees an instant flash of some actual car. Your mind reacts the same way to abstract thoughts like love or success. There's an instant image, or picture, flashed on the screen of your mind which illustrates love or success as you understand it.

This mental picture can be either vivid or lifeless, depending on how well your powers of imagination are developed. Now notice that Proverbs 23:7 could be read, "As he pictures or imagines in his heart, so is he."

With this in mind you can see that the self-image theory goes something like this: Whatever pictures or images are held in the mind often enough and long enough tend to work out in fully developed reality. Exactly what is often enough and long enough varies from person to person and project to project.

I know of a little girl, once 11 years old, who daily accompanied her preacher-father to a radio station back in the 1930s, when most radio music was live. A giant pipe organ was one of the reasons this child was eager to go with her father to his six-day-per-week program. She did not go to see or hear her father preach. It was that great, white, gold-trimmed organ console and its wide range of resonant tones of beautiful music that fascinated her. But the breathtaking knowledge that the organist would let her sit on the bench with him as he played was what really enchanted her. For that half-hour she was "Alice-in-organland." In her mind she played that mighty Wurlitzer every time she sat with her charming musical prince.

A church near her father's had a giant instrument too, much like the one at the radio station. It was considerably larger, in every way, than the one in her dad's church. She was allowed to play on her own church organ, but she frequently sneaked off to see the one close by, sitting in the balcony with her legs swinging rhythmically as she imagined she was the church organist playing the selection then being practiced by the organist.

She vowed that she would be an organist when she grew up. It was a vow that she held in her mind constantly, even though she never owned an organ in her life; it was always someone else's organ on which she could play or practice. She never had a lesson, but she did have an image of herself as an organist.

She never got big, for even today she is a petite 125 pounds and quite slender. But she is a great organist who has thrilled thousands with her unique style, which is so distinct that when people who know her walk into an auditorium where she is playing, they say, "That's Ginny."

The self-image she held in her mind so long became a reality in spite of many hindrances. She held the mental picture . . . she believed . . . she worked. Finally the day came when she was the staff organist in the big church where, as a child, her dream began. I know the story well. I've heard it often. Ginny is my wife!

The problem that bothers me and turns on a bright yellow caution light in my mind is the undeniable fact that the self-image theory, like its twin, self-love, starts with man and builds inward in a cyclical fashion, often tending to be concerned with self more than with others. It becomes a me-and-my-rights, me-and-my-goals syndrome. This is more humanistic than scriptural. This contradicts the "others-orientation" of Christ's way of life. If we follow Him perfectly we must be concerned about others more than we are about ourselves.

The Scriptures are quite explicit about this fact. Over 60 times the New Testament speaks of ministering to and caring for one another. The early church was a one-another church. Note the emphasis that Paul puts on our obligation to others:

> Bear ye one another's burdens, and so fulfill the law of Christ (Galatians 6:2).

> We then that are strong ought to bear the infirmities of the weak, and not to please ourselves. Let every one of us please his neighbor for his good, to edification. For even Christ pleased not himself, but, as it is written, "The reproaches of them that reproached thee fell on me" (Romans 15:1-3).

> For I say, through the grace given unto me, to every man that is among you, not to think of himself more highly than he ought to think,but to think soberly, according as God hath dealt to every man the measure of faith (Romans 12:3).

> Let nothing be done through strife or vainglory, but in lowliness of mind let each esteem others better than themselves. Look not every man on his own things, but every man also on the things of others. Let this mind be in you which was also in Christ Jesus, who, being in the form of God, thought it not robbery to be equal with God, but made himself of no reputation, and took upon him the form of a servant, and was made in the likeness of men; and being found in fashion as a man, he humbled himself, and became obedient unto death, even the death of the cross. Wherefore God also hath highly exalted him, and given him a name which is above every name, that at the name of Jesus every knee should bow, of things in heaven, and things in earth, and things under the earth, and that every tongue should confess that Jesus Christ is Lord, to the glory of God the Father (Philippians 2:3-11).

Note carefully this Philippians passage. Verses 3-5 tell us to be lowly minded, esteeming others better than ourselves. We should not look on our own things but should rather concern ourselves about the welfare of others, for this was the attitude that Jesus took.

The force of this exhortation is intensified when it is understood that Jesus was equal to His Father (v.6) and it would not be amiss for Him to claim this for Himself. But instead of doing so, He did just the opposite (v.7). He made Himself of no reputaton and chose to take the position of a *slave* (literal Greek). He humbled Himself even to permitting Himself to be killed like a criminal, when in fact He was totally without sin. Paul recommends this attitude to us.

That attitude hardly fits today's concept of a "good self-image," but it is the standard we are urged to have for our selves (v.5). God displayed His approval and acceptance of this attitude held in Jesus' mind (vv. 9, 10). Note the "wherefore," which points backward to Christ's self-abasement and forward to the fact that this is the basis on which God exalted Jesus to the highest place in the universe. He also gave Him a name above every name, at which every knee shall bow and every tongue confess that He is Lord of lords and King of kings, to the eternal honor and glory of God.

This is a perfect commentary on the words of Jesus recorded in Mark 8:35, telling us that to "lose our lives" is the way to discover what God has designed us to be, but to preserve our lives is to shut the door to a true version of what we can really become. Christ's greatest work was accomplished through total refusal to claim His own prerogatives. Instead, He put the welfare of others in first place. He knew quite well who He was. He knew He was the perfect likeness of God, the express image of His Person (Hebrews 1:3 and John 14:7-9). But what was more important to Him than that was what *others* could become if He would sacrifice Himself for them. He knew that every man was created in, and still bore, the likeness and image of God. He fully understood man's flawed, damaged, sinful status. But He also knew that man was redeemable and restorable. Furthermore, He knew that all who believe in Him are predestined to be conformed to the same image He bore. So to redeem and restore them He humbled Himself and became like one of us so that we could be like Him.

It is interesting to study the process by which sinful man is restored into the likeness and image of his Creator. First he must acknowledge that he has sinned and fallen short of what he was designed to be. Then he must accept the gift of eternal life offered to him by trusting in and relying on the fact that Jesus, the infinite god-man, has died for his sin. Having turned his back on his former way of life by repentance, he enters into a process of change from what he formerly was, to what he eventually shall be: like Jesus, who is the perfect likeness and image of God (Romans 8:29).

This process is in two phases. The first is lifelong; it is a gradual, step-at-a-time, bit-by-bit process as the Holy Spirit and the Word of God are effectively applied to that person's life. A one-verse description of this lengthy but effective process is 2 Corinthians 3:18:

> But we all with open face beholding as in a glass the glory of the Lord are changed into the same image from glory to glory, even as by the Spirit of the Lord.

The second phase is climactic, instantaneous, and total. It happens when the dead in Christ are resurrected and the living believers are caught up at the second coming of Christ. 1 Corinthians 15:51-54 and I John 3:1, 2 spell this out in detail.

> Behold, I show you a mystery: We shall not all sleep, but we shall all be changed, in a moment, in the twinkling of an eye, at the last trump; for the trumpet shall sound, and the dead shall be raised incorruptible, and we shall be changed. For this corruptible must put on incorruption, and this mortal must put on immortality. So when this corruptible

shall have put on incorruption, and this mortal shall have put on immortality, then shall be brought to pass the saying that is written, Death is swallowed up in victory.

Behold what manner of love the Father hath bestowed upon us, that we should be called the sons of God; therefore the world knoweth us not, because it knew him not. Beloved, now are we the sons of God, and it doth not yet appear what we shall be; but we know that, when he shall appear we shall be like him, for we shall see him as he is.

But it is the *first* phase of this process that is important to this discussion of the self-image doctrine. There we see the principle in action as intended by God.

According to 2 Corinthians 3:18 (quoted above), as we hold thoughts (mental pictures) of who and what Jesus is, we are changed into His image, a step at a time, from glory to glory—from one wonderful thing to another.

God knew the end from the beginning when He created mankind. He made Adam and Eve in His own likeness and image. He also knew that man could damage that image, and man did. But God had a plan designed to correct the resulting flaw. Part of that plan included designing man so that the mental images (thoughts) held in his mind would tend to control and mold that man. He also arranged things so that man could be taught to keep Jesus in his mind. As a result man could be restored to the glory for which he was created.

I believe that is why God commands us to love Him with all our hearts, all our minds, and all our strength. To enable us to obey this command He gave us Jesus (who is the express image of His person) to die for our sins, thus showing us how much He cares for us and loves us. The net result of all this is that as we behold His love for us in Jesus' birth, death, resurrection, ascension, and present ministry in, for, and to us, we are gradually changed back into the image in which we were created.

That's what the self-image potential is all about. That's why we have this built-in-capacity to be transformed by the mental pictures we hold in our minds. This is our glorious potential. But right here is also the potential error that will destroy us if we misuse it.

Let's examine one of the potential dangers. What about the person who really believes in the power of the self-image dynamic, but never uses it for its God-designed purpose? Instead, he creates his own self-image if what he wants to be, setting his own goals with never a thought about what God wants.

Such a person might just as well carve an image of wood or ivory and take it to God and ask Him to bless it. God doesn't bless idols. This introduces the peril of developing a self-image contrary to God's plan for man.

God's Word tells us that we are not to have any gods before Him. He also says that we are to seek His kingdom and His righteousness *first*. So the peril to be wary of in the self-image doctrine is that of misusing a God-given faculty—for self aggrandizement or a selfish purpose instead of that for which it was intended.

Recognizing the danger just mentioned does not close the matter. There are many other questions. One question about self-image that needs an answer is this: Is it ever proper to use the self-image principle for purposes other than to conform one's self to the image of Jesus Christ?

The answer is yes. It is a matter of priorities. When one seeks to be like Jesus *first*, when that is his *prime* goal, when this overrides any and all other goals, I believe it is not only proper to do so, but there is an obligation to do so. For example, a Christian salesman should be as good as his craft as it is possible for him to be. This requires that he have a good self-image of himself as a salesman. Christian salespeople should be the best in the business. This goes for arts, crafts, professions, skills, and careers of all kind. We should strive to be 110 percent of our potential at all times, thus stretching our potential and growing daily.

The problem is always the same—priorities! We need to keep God first, others second, and self third. One of the best ways to accomplish this is to quit thinking in terms of having a "good" self-image. Instead, think in terms of an *accurate* self-image.

Note the difference—self-image is generally an evaluation that someone makes about himself and, being a human evaluation, it is subject to human error. Thus a person with a poor self-image may be comparing himself to false standards. He may be better than that by which he compares himself, or he may be worse. There is vast room for error unless our standards and our knowledge of ourselves are accurate. We need absolute universals and totally accurate self-knowledge to be sure our self-evaluation is correct.

I have given up striving for a self-image that seems good to me. I am now concerned about having an *accurate* self-image. I want to see myself as God sees me. Then I will never be inaccurate. What I see may be bad, but it will be accurate.

I know that God sees me has having been created in His likeness and image. That is accurate but it is bad, for He also sees me as a flawed, sinful image, quite unlike what He created man to be. That's really bad, but it is accurate. He sees that I am repairable, potentially like Jesus. That is good, and accurate. God is faithful, having begun a good work in me (restoring me to the original likeness in which man was created). He will complete it (Philippians 1:6). That is also good. I have failed and will fail again. That is bad, but accurate. However, I know that God has made a provision for this (1 John 1:9):

> If we confess our sins, he is faithful and just to forgive us our sins, and to cleanse us from all unrighteousness.

The Bible is full of data about man. There is no need to be surprised at any depth to which he may fall or any height to which he can rise. God is able to keep us from falling and to make us stand in any situation. But if He lets man alone, there sees to be no bottom to the pit into which he slides.

When people I counsel tell me how worthless they are, I always agree. I even tell them that they would probably feel worse if they knew how bad off they are as compared to what they could be in Christ. I then show them that God has a plan to transform them into the image of His Son. We start building and rebuilding from that point. I will never try to repair their own bad self-image. I try to get them to have a funeral for it. I try to get them to see themselves as God sees them—both as fallen, sinful creatures and as creatures that can become like Him.

Accepting a counselee's bad evaluation of himself seems to give him confidence that I understand his plight. Formerly, when I tried to convince the counselee that he was not as bad as he thought, I frequently heard things like, "No one seems to understand how I feel." By that I knew he thought that neither did I understand. Now that I accept his poor self-evaluation and suggest that it is probably even worse, the counselee believes I take him seriously. Then, when I tell him there is hope, he believes I'm still serious. I find that this is a confidence-building procedure rather than a deterrent. Seeing oneself through God's eyes is the only truly safe use of the self-image doctrine.

12

Transpersonal Psychology

Transpersonal Psychology is the latest study of man to achieve academic status in the psychological field. However, it has been in the periphery for a long time. Mark Cosgrove identifies its subject matter as

> . . . expanded consciousness and the spiritual nature of man via drugs, meditation, biofeedback, deep hypnosis, ESP, occult topics, deathbed experiences, and Eastern religions (*Psychology Gone Awry*, Zondervan).

The name "transpersonal" suggests what it is all about. The prefix "trans-" means "across; beyond; through; surpassing; transcending."

Stated more simply, "transpersonal" means to go beyond the normal state of mind in which man functions. Transpersonal psychologists try to see man in altered states of consciousness; they study man's mental experiences when he is under the influence of drugs or is in deep meditation, or what his experiences are in any of the mental states created by the other factors mentioned by Dr. Cosgrove. What is important in these studies is not what happens to the man physically, but rather what happens experientially in his mental awareness.

Aldous Huxley argued if man could escape himself—get outside himself—he could find reality. Apparently he felt that man's prejudices, developed over the years, had blinded him to real truth. The real truth, Huxley seems to have said, is there in man's head, but he cannot get to it because of self-imposed limitations. All that is needed is to alter his conscious awareness and get him off on a hallucinatory trip so that he can find a higher, truer reality than he now experiences.

That roughly speaking, is what transpersonal psychology is all about. This is not a full definition, but it does point to the direction it is headed.

In 1969 the *Journal of Transpersonal Psychology* defined its field of interest this way:

> The Journal of Transpersonal Psychology is concerned with . . . metaneeds, ultimate values, unitive consciousness, peak experiences, ecstasy, mystical experience, B values, essence, bliss, awe, wonder, self-actualization, ultimate meaning, transcendence of the self, spirit, sacralization of everyday life, oneness, cosmic awareness, cosmic play, individual and species-wide synergy, maximal interpersonal encounter, transcendental phenomena, maximal sensory awareness, responsiveness and expression; and related concepts, experiences and activities.

Note that every area listed involves metaphysical things, beyond what is normal to basic knowledge. They call it ultimate reality, or higher states of "true" awareness.

As mentioned earlier, this way of thinking is not new. It was here at the turn of the twentieth century. William James and Karl Jung also wrote of some of these states of awareness. Jung was deeply interested in dreams. The late Abraham Maslow, a prominent and influential humanistic psychologist of the recent decade, did much to give transpersonal psychology academic credibiity. In the same Journal quoted above, he said:

> Thus we are using techniques for selecting the most fully developed, the most fully human persons we can find and

suggesting that these people are what the whole human species can be like if you just let them grow, if the conditions are good and you get out of their way.

Maslow went on to report "peak experiences" in which a person is in a moment of bliss and is egoless, beyond time and space, good and evil. He observed that these states were similar to what had often been reported about people under the influence of drugs and meditation *(Psychology Gone Awry,* Chapter VII).

This principle is carried so far that at least one psychoanalyst, R.D. Laing, compares what happens in insane patients suffering from extreme identity loss with the experiences that certain mystics had observed in people. Thus the idea has developed that insane people may be experiencing truer reality than normal people experience. Maybe, according to them, those peope we now call psychotic are nearer true normality than are the rest of us. This reasoning is also part of Transpersonal Psychology.

To the uniniated this way of thinking seems ecrie, far out, and difficult to grasp. This is because it is wedded to Eastern religion, which is almost totally foreign to Western culture. This mixture of East and West is too complicated for a Westerner to easily grasp, but enough of the problem can be described to identify it.

First, Western culture tends to emphasize the individual and his separateness from other individuals. Each person is an entity in himself. But Eastern religious thought emphasizes the unity of all persons. They think everything flows out of a cosmic universal mind. If you can imagine a great mental ocean out of which flows rivers and streams of consciousness, with all mankind connected to that great psychic ocean by these little streams and each person being one with it and therefore one is everyone and everything else, then you have an oversimplified model of Eastern religious unity. At death an individual's consciousness flows back into the oceanic awareness from which it came, and the individual ceases to exist. Then the consciousness flows out again into something else, or someone else, in a sort of reincarnation principle.

Second, this Eastern thought believes that all matter—rocks, trees, even all *things* in general—have moral qualities. These things are and teach physical expressions of thought. They are less real than the thought they illustrate or portray.

If this leaves you with a frustrated sense of "lostness" and bewilderment, wait until you try to grasp the whole ideology! Then you will begin to see the true complexity of the entire psychology.

The true transpersonal psychologist, however, believes in both the Western and Eastern approach to reality, each separate from the other. Cosgrove, with characteristic clearness, defines these two in a chapter titled "The Nature of Reality."

> The Nature of Reality—
> To the transpersonal psychologist reality is "two-headed," one head represented by the Western view of a physical, orderly world, and the other by the Eastern view of the spiritual oneness of reality. On the Western side we have stars, planets, people, and atoms, all ruled by principles of cause and effect. On the Eastern side we have universal mind and spiritual substance, which operate by non-casual principles, infusing all matter. The non-causal principles, of the spiritual side of the universe give rise to magical, coincidental, and illogical effects.

One of these illogical effects comes from blending these two opposites. The transpersonal psychologist tends to give more validity to the Eastern view than to the Western, for to him the Western materialistic approach to reality is less important than the Eastern. The West's cause-and-effect universe of things, like the sun, moon, planets, and stars, as well as entities like people, is less important than the mental oneness of the Eastern philosophies.

This not only seems *illogical* to the Western mind, but it

seems impossible. Maybe this is what Kipling meant when he said,

> East is East
> and West is West,
> and never the twain shall meet.

This is an adequate analysis of transpersonal psychology, but it is enough of an introduction to identify the fact that it is complex and difficult.

Since it has become academically acceptable and attracts the attention of some great names in psychology, and is a strong "Fourth Force," it behooves students to know about it.

If we want to refute its fundamental concepts we will need students who are well-acquainted with the absolutes of the Bible and are firmly grounded in those scriptural truths. These students can then study this fourth force without being overwhelmed by it and can become the new leaders, placing God's truth where it belongs—the foundation and capstone of all truth.

13

Philosophy and Psychology

Now it is time to take a look at the soil and roots out of which psychology has grown. Earlier I pointed to the fact that three major forces have had a powerful impact in psychology: philosophy, empiricism, and evolution.

Philosophy can accurately be defined as a formal study of reality: reality of things in general or of some specialized section of reality. It comes from two Greek words: *philo*, which means love, and *sophia*, which is insight into the true nature of things.

The value of wisdom is undisputed. It is priceless. But many people think of wisdom as *tact*. Tact is a quick or intuitive appreciation of what is fit, or proper, or right; especially, it is skill in avoiding that which might offend or disturb. It is being considerate of the feelings and needs of others.

To better see the difference, just realize that a man could be tactful and yet have little or no insight into the true reality of things. Or he could have deep insights into reality but be tactless in his use of those insights. Tactfulness is a good companion for wisdom. They make a wonderful team. But they are far from being the same thing.

It is important to make the above distinction and to remember that the word "wisdom" (philosophy) as used here refers to true insight into the reality of things as they are.

God *wants* His creatures to have insight into the true nature of everything. This is clearly taught in the Book of Proverbs.

Proverbs 4:5-9—
Get wisdom, get understanding; forget it not, neither decline from the words of my mouth.

Forsake her not, and she shall preserve thee; love her, and she shall keep thee.

Wisdom is the principal thing; therefore get wisdom, and with all thy getting get understanding.

Exalt her, and she shall promote thee; she shall bring thee to honor when thou dost embrace her.

She shall give to thine head an ornament of grace; a crown of glory shall she deliver to thee.

Proverbs 3:13-18—
Happy is the man that findeth wisdom, and the man that getteth understanding.

For the merchandise of it is better than the merchandise of silver, and the gain thereof than fine gold.

She is more precious than rubies; and all the things thou canst desire are not to be compared unto her.

Length of days is in her right hand, and in her left hand riches and honor.

Her ways are ways of pleasantness, and all her paths are peace.

She is a tree of life to them that lay hold upon her, and happy is everyone that retaineth her.

In Proverbs chapters 7, 8, and 9 are strong appeals urging upon mankind the value and virtue of wisdom. Personified as a woman, wisdom is portrayed in these chapters as crying out to mankind, pleading with them to realize that "wisdom," the insight into true reality, is far more valuable than any other thing.

Proverbs 8:11—
For wisdom is better than rubies, and all things that may be desired are not to be compared to it.

A study of the Proverbs' references to wisdom will bring a valuable asset into any man's store of knowledge. Wisdom is the prime subject of this amazing book.

Paul in his Letter to the Corinthians, makes a distinction between the wisdom of this world and the wisdom of God (1 Corinthians 1:20,21; 2:5-7). His argument is that man, in his approach to wisdom, has failed to include God; therefore, this human wisdom turns into foolishness. Because of people's rejection of God, Paul warns that God will destroy *their* wisdom, and show it to be folly.

James 3:13-17 has something to say about wisdom:

> Who among you is wise and understanding? Let him show by his good behavior his deeds in the gentleness of wisdom.

> But if you have bitter jealousy and selfish ambition in your heart, do not be arrogant and so lie against the truth.

> This wisdom is not that which comes down from above, but is earthly, natural, demonic.

> For where jealousy and selfish ambition exist, there is disorder and every evil thing.

> But the wisdom from above is first pure, then peaceable, gentle, reasonable, full of mercy and good fruits, unwavering, without hypocrisy (NASB).

Note that both James and Paul made a distinction between two kinds of wisdom: that which is *not* from above and that which *is* from above. He also gives some guidelines to tell which is which.

Not everything that parades as wisdom is necessarily true wisdom. It is possible for something to be called love of wisdom or philosophy but actually be—

a vain deceit,
the traditions of men,

the rudiments of the world (Colossians 2:8),
demonic, earthly, and natural (James 3:15).

Paul makes it clear that this sort of philosophy will *spoil* a person:

> Beware lest any man spoil you through philosophy and vain deceit, after the traditions of men, after the rudiments of this world, and not after Christ (Colossians 2:8).

This word "spoil" appears only once in the New Testament *(sulagogeo)*, but it is a pungent word. It means to rob and carry away into slavery. As the apostle uses it here the reader is warned that to try to comprehend the reality of things (philosophy) without including Jesus Christ is to fall victim to "the wisdom of the world" and what James said was "earthly, natural (as opposed to spiritual), and demonic." This will rob a man of the truth about reality and lead him into the slavery of falsehood.

Paul argues that all the treasures of wisdom and knowledge are "hidden in Christ." He further warns that it is possible to be deceived by enticing words of man's wisdom:

> **Colossians 2:2-4—**
> That their hearts might be comforted, being knit together in love, and unto all riches of the full assurance of understanding, to the acknowledgment of the mystery of God, and of the Father, and of Christ,
>
> In whom are hid all the treasures of wisdom and knowledge.
>
> And this I say, lest any man should beguile you with enticing words.

But in heeding the warning about being spoiled by philosophy or beguiled by enticing words, one does not necessarily have to avoid hearing or reading the enticing words of man's or the world's philosophies. He can do that and still be ignorant and vulnerable to error. The dangers Paul sees are circumvented by being rooted in and built up in Christ Jesus, and established by faith in Him.

As will be pointed out later, the more we know about the world's philosophy, the better equipped we are to deal with it. Being ignorant of what natural philosophy says is not an asset if one is interested in showing and refuting its errors. If one is fully rooted and established in Christ Jesus and stays in the faith, he will be a sharper instrument by knowing what the world's philosophy has to say. Buf if he lets it turn him away from Christ it will spoil him.

Paul avoided saying anything that might detract from Jesus Christ or do anything that kept men from clearly seeing who and what *He* was and what *He* could do for them.

1 Corinthians 1:17-31; 2:1-8—

For Christ sent me not to baptize, but to preach the gospel: not with wisdom of words, lest the cross of Christ should be made of none effect.

For the preaching of the cross is to them that perish foolishness, but unto us which are saved it is the power of God.

For it is written, I will destroy the wisdom of the wise, and will bring to nothing the understanding of the prudent.

Where is the wise? Where is the scribe? Where is the disputer of this world? Hath not God made foolish the wisdom of this world?

For after that in the wisdom of God the world by wisdom knew not God, it pleased God by the foolishness of preaching to save them that believe.

For the Jews require a sign, and the Greeks seek after wisdom,

But we preach Christ crucified, unto the Jews a stumbling block, and unto the Greeks foolishness,

But unto them which are called, both Jews and Greeks, Christ the power of God and the wisdom of God.

Because the foolishness of God is wiser than men, and the weakness of God is stronger than men.

For ye see your calling, brethren, how that not many wise men after the flesh, not many mighty, not many noble, are called;

But God hath chosen the foolish things of the world to confound the wise; and God hath chosen the weak things of the world to confound the things which are mighty,

And base things of the world, and things which are despised, hath God chosen, yea, and things which are not, to bring to nought things that are,

That no flesh should glory in his presence.

But of him are ye in Christ, Jesus, who of God is made unto us wisdom, and righteousness, and sanctification, and redemption.

That according as it is written, He that glorieth, let him glory in the Lord.

And I, brethren, when I came to you, came not with excellency of speech or wisdom, declaring unto you the testimony of God.

For I determined not to know anything among you, save Jesus Christ, and him crucified.

And I was with you in weakness, and in fear, and in much trembling.

And my speech and my preaching was not with enticing words of man's wisdom, but in demonstration of the Spirit and of power,

> That your faith should not stand in the wisdom of men, but in the power of God.

> Howbeit we speak wisdom among them that are perfect: yet not the wisdom of this world, nor of the princes of this world, that come to nought,

> But we speak the wisdom of God in a mystery, even the hidden wisdom, which God ordained before the world unto our glory.

To Paul, Christ was the Wisdom of God. In Him one can find the insights that make true reality available and understandable. This was because Jesus makes God more understandable, and that is because He *is* God in human form. He *is* Immanuel, God with us.

It is interesting to recall that the world's wisdom of Paul's day is of little value in correcting error today. Most of the world's wisdom of that era now seems hopelessly inadequate as a guide for living in our culture. Most of it was the big thing then, but few people pay any attention to it now. That is because they left the reality of God out of their knowledge. What Paul warned about came to pass—

> For it is written, "I will destroy the wisdom of the wise, and the cleverness of the clever I will set aside."

> Where is the wise man? Where is the scribe? Where is the debater of this age? Has not God made foolish the wisdom of the world? (1 Corinthians 1:19,20 NASB).

Miles of shelves loaded with books that no one pays attention to (as in the Library of Paris) testify to what happens to the wisdom of man. But the Christ-centered wisdom that Paul preached is still valid, still influencing millions of lives, still the foundation of all moral society. That is because Paul's philosophy was based on the personal God as revealed by Jesus Christ.

The wisdom of this world that Paul wrote about is the wisdom I have identified as one of the roots of psychology. The results are obvious.

Paul uses a metaphor in Romans 11:16 that is appropriate to this discussion. He uses an olive tree's roots and branches to illustrate a truth about Abraham (the root) and Israel (the branches). He wrote:

> . . . If the root be holy, so are the branches.

In so saying he implies that the opposite is also true:

> . . . If the root is *unholy*, so are the branches.

The wisdom of this world that has left the personal, communicating God of the Bible out of its knowledge is an *unholy* root and has corrupted its branches.

Any insights into the realities about man that omit God are inadequate to explain man. Leaving God out leaves vital questions unanswered. Most psychologies ignore these unanswered questions rather than admit God's existence as answers to them.

This is not the place to discuss all these psychological questions that remain unanswered because God is rejected, or to explain how keeping Him in one's quest for knowledge gives complete answers. That is in itself a mammoth task.

For that purpose of this book's message it is enough to know that—

> There is no wisdom nor understanding nor counsel against the Lord (Proverbs 20:31).

Therefore, any teaching that is against the Lord—that denies His existence, Person, or communication—is the wisdom of this world and is to be rejected.

14

Empiricism and Psychology

Another root through which modern psychology has drawn its form is called empiricism. This is the doctrine that all knowledge is derived from sensory experience. It teaches reliance on sensory observation and experiment as the only true basis of knowledge.

In other words, unless a subject can be seen, touched, tasted, smelled, or heard; or experimented with; or is manipulatable; or can be measured or weighed and thus shown to have substance, it is considered as nonexistent, not factual, not truly real, and therefore unknowable.

Another term akin to but not identical to empiricism is scientism, which means adherence to the aims and methods of scientists. A scientist is one who studies knowledge by investigations which have been logically arranged and systematizied in the form of a hypothesis which is rigorously subjected to all known laws of verification, which in turn requires exact observation.

If that seems complicated, wait until you hear that the two, empiricism and scientism, are married into something called scientific empiricism. This newly wedded pair is also called logical positivism.

Positivism is a way of thinking that regards nothing as ascertained or, for that matter, ascertainable at all except that which can be examined by physical, sensory perception. It holds that man can have no knowledge of anything unless it is directly observable as an object, or an action, or a verifiable change. It rejects speculation concerning origins or causes, since these causes cannot be duplicated and examined. To a scientific empirical positivist, these methods alone give certitude to knowledge.

But there is a problem with this system. First, by this method God cannot be known. Second, for the same reason there is much about man that cannot be studied. More about these two problems later.

However, the two problems mentioned are not enough reason to reject the total empirical, scientific, positivistic systems. In many areas of knowledge they are highly desirable.

For example, if a surgeon is going to operate on me I want him to have learned his surgical skills and knowledge by rigorous application of all three systems of obtaining skills and knowledge. Of course I'd feel better about the whole affair if the doctor also knew God on a personal basis. But knowing God would not make up for lack of surgical skill if he is going to operate on me. Some scientifically developed knowledge and ability is necessary, as far as I am concerned.

The same thing is true about airplanes that I pilot. I want the engineers and craftsmen who build the plane to have diligently applied all scientific skills known to aeronautical engineering in designing and constructing the ship.

Or if I'm a passenger on a commercial airline I want the pilots and engineers to be thoroughly scientific in the way they fly and otherwise control the planes. I hope, too, that there was no neglect in scientific, empirical positivism in the training of these men.

There isn't enough space in this book to discuss all of the benefits of scientific methods that make our lives easier and more pleasant. The technologies in farming, radio, television, automobiles, construction, marketing, and thousands of other areas have helped develop an era of prosperity unequaled in the history of the world.

But with all this unprecedented prosperity a serious problem has developed, for by the methods of scientific empiricism and positivism God cannot be discovered. Job knew this when he asked, "Canst thou by searching find out God?" (Job 11:7).

That is a question with only one answer: *no.* God cannot be observed by the human senses. He cannot be manipulated or experimented with by laboratory procedures. He cannot be measured or weighed. Because He cannot be examined in this way, He is considered to be nonexistent. Or if He exists, He is considered unknowable.

This is one of the roots through which psychology has drawn its body of knowledge. Joined to the root just described in the last chapter (the wisdom or philosophy of this world, which also leaves God out of its data) we see a twin source of error: godless empiricism and godless philosophy.

There is no justifiable excuse for these errors, because all the information necessary to understand God's eternal existence, His power, and His headship over creation is clearly displayed and made understandable by that creation.

> Because that which may be known of God is manifest in them, for God hath showed it unto them.
>
> For the invisible things of him from the creation of the world are clearly seen, being understood by the things that are made, even his eternal power and Godhead, so that they are without excuse (Romans 1:19,20).

Psalm 19 puts it this way:

> The heavens declare the glory of God, and the firmament showeth his handiwork.
>
> Day unto day uttereth speech, and night unto night showeth knowledge.
>
> There is no speech nor language where their voice is not heard.

> Their line is go out through all the earth, and their words to the end of the world. In them hath he set a tabernacle for the sun,
>
> Which is as a bridegroom coming out of his chamber and rejoiceth as a strong man to run a race (Psalm 19:1-5).

As Paul said in Acts 14:15,17), ". . . the living God, who made heaven and earth and the sea and all things that are therein . . . left not Himself without witness."

And what a compelling witness it is! The intricacy of the universe defies any explanation other than the fact that a powerful, highly intelligent Being brought it into existence.

It is sheer folly to believe that random chance plus time could bring a delicate watch into existence without an intelligent designer and maker. It is no less foolish to say that the world or its universe just happened apart from a Creator.

The world is God's creation and we are His creatures, made in His likeness and image. God demands that we know who and what He is so that we can know who and what we are. Failure to acknowledge Him is the fatal flaw faced by all mankind in all eras.

Francis Schaeffer's writings include two books that brilliantly discuss God's existence and the fact that He has spoken to man. The titles tell the message of each book: *The God Who Is There* (InterVarsity) and *He Is There And He Is Not Silent*" (Tyndale). To read them is to be enriched.

God has indeed spoken to man "at sundry times and in diverse manners" by the prophets and "hath in these last days spoken to us by His Son," Jesus Christ (Hebrews 1:1).

Romans 1:18-32 forcefully tells us the results that develop when man leaves God out of his knowledge. One could hardly conceive a more exact description of the culture in which we find ourselves, for many of our scientists and our philosophers have rejected God, or have refused to acknowledge

Him. Many of our psychologies have also submitted to and absorbed the same error. We are reaping the predicted harvest.

It is proper to again point to the fact that not all psychologists have submitted to this error. Many have not. But the "four forces" in psychology mentioned in this book have done so, and anyone who uses their materials needs to screen it well lest the viewpoints they find therein turn out to be perverse.

I believe that a true Christian position should be—

> To the law and to the testimony: if they speak not according to this word, it is because there is no light in them (Isaiah 8:20).

I do not reject empirical or scientific methods of research where they deal with material, physical subjects. But I thoroughly resist the system that says that if something is not examinable by their methods, then it does not exist as knowledge. This epistemology is erroneous.

The real problem has been well-identified by Paul in his Letters to the Corinthians.

> But the natural man receiveth not the things of the Spirit of God, for they are foolishness unto him; neither can he know them, because they are spiritually discerned (1 Corinthians 2:14).

> But if our gospel be hid, it is hid to them that are lost, in whom the god of this world hath blinded the minds of them which believe not, lest the light of the glorious gospel of Christ, who is the image of God, should shine unto them (2 Corinthians 4:4).

The natural man of 1 Corinthians 2:14 is spiritually dead and cannot properly respond to the things of the Spirit of God. He is blind to the light of this.

However, the person who is spiritually dead can have a

rebirth and can receive new life—he can believe if he chooses to do so. God's offer is open to all. He will give eternal, spiritual life to all who believe and receive the good news about Jesus Christ, who died and rose again that we might have eternal life.

15

Evolution and Psychology

Neither one of the two roots of psychology already discussed is as corrupt as this one. Evolution has done more to damage humanity and carry people away from the Bible than has any other academic pursuit.

Evolution has been almost universally accepted as an absolute reality. Many evolutionists believe it to be a proven fact that life came out of nothing, spontaneously. Then slowly, over millions of years, life evolved from stage to stage, from a protozoan to an amoeba, then to a worm, to a fish, to an amphibian, to a reptile, to a fowl, to a mammal, and finally to a man. (This theory is less popular now, but thousands of textbooks still proclaim it as a scientific fact.)

People are often deemed illiterate or ignorant if they refuse to accept evolution as an adequate explanation of the origin of life in the many species of flora and fauna, including man.

Data have been gathered, sorted, classified, and unified. Museums have been crowded with fossils and skeletons which are displayed with supportive pictures and charts in an overwhelming array that portrays the history of the evolution of man. It is indeed impressive.

Evolutionists argue that the facts of biology, the facts of embryology, the facts of paleontology, and the facts of anthropology prove that evolution is a fact. But that is simply untrue: Evolution is only a theory; it is not a fact. It is a hypothesis: a guess. The facts mentioned above have not lifted it above the hypothetical, theoretical levels of knowledge. This is because no known facts clarify the questions that challenge the validity of the evolution hypothesis.

Evolution, in spite of the titanic mass of data used to support it, is vulnerable to serious problems that thoroughly discredit it.

One of these problems is the question of where life came from in the first place. Some evolutionists believe that life may have come from outer space on a meteor that crashed onto the earth's surface millions or trillions of years ago. At least one scientist has suggested that living organisms may have been planted here by visitors from outer space who arrived in what we now think of as UFOs. That doesn't fully answer the question. It merely transfers it to another base. How did it get on the meteor or the UFO? Where was it before that? Where did it come from in the first place?

There are no answers to these questions that will satisfy the accepted methods of scientific research, for it cannot be demonstrated or proven in laboratory conditions. Therefore, evolution remains unproven: merely a hypothesis and not a fact.

God's Word tells us that creation can be understood by ONLY ONE METHOD, and that method is faith.

> Through faith we understand that the worlds were framed by the word of God, so that things which are seen were not made of things which do appear (Hebrews 11:3).

Both atheist evolutionists and Christian creationists must accept their ideas about creation by faith—it's merely a matter of which idea is more credible. And the evidence for creation is far more credible than that used to support evolution.

There are other theories about the origin of life, some of which say it came spontaneously, of its own accord. Other theorists believe that life was caused by a cosmic eruption of some kind. But they also have the same difficulties mentioned above.

The whole theory of evolution would receive a highly destructive blow if the spontaneous generation of life could be shown to be highly improbable, or that life coming from any nonintelligent, nonplanning source is completely farfetched.

What are the probabilities in favor of reproducible life coming into existence unaided by a highly intelligent power that can think and plan and has the energy to execute the plan?

What is the probability that random parts could come together in highly specific order? For example, suppose we have ten ping pong balls numbered from one to ten. We put them in a box and mix them up. Then we ask a blindfolded person to draw them out, one at a time, in the following fashion.

This blindfolded person must reach into the box and on the first draw pick up ping pong ball number one. This is recorded and the ball returned to the box and remingled with the others. Next he reaches in and must on the second draw get ball number two and return it to the box. After this is recorded he reaches in again. This time ball number three must be extracted and returned to the box. And so on until ten draws have been made. The question is, What is the probability that the person could at random draw out of the box the ping pong balls numbered one through ten in that order, and in only ten draws?

The law of probabilities is formed as follows. In each draw there is one chance in ten of getting the right ball in the right order. The equation for each draw is 1/10 (one chance in ten possibilities) that it will happen, and 10/1 that it won't. For the ten draws in this illustration the formula is $1/10^{10}$, or, $1/10 \times 1/10 \times 1/10 \times 1/10 \times 1/10 \times 1/10 \times 1/10 \times 1/10 \times 1/10 \times 1/10$, or one to the 10th power. Multiply all the ones on top of the fraction and you still have one. Multiply the tens below the line and you have 100,000,000,000, (one hundred billion). So the probability that this drawing of ten balls, numbered one through ten, in that order, and with only ten draws, is one hundred billion to one that it will not happen.

What has this to do with reproducible life being produced by chance? It illustrates how the probabilities are developed.

Life which will reproduce itself is (in its smallest form) a cell so tiny that many cells could be put on the head of a pin. One cell can be examined only by the use of a microscope. If we could expand that cell until it was large enough for us to get inside it, we would learn that is composed of over 400 parts! Then we would learn that there is high specificity in the order of those parts.

Just how complex this specificity is can be learned from a molecule of hemoglobin, the complex respiratory pigment in the blood's red corpuscles. In this molecule alone are collected about 200 units in such specific order that if one unit is out of place it causes an illness known as sickle cell anemia. This is a violently painful, fatal blood disease.

Even so, biochemists now know from their studies of DNA (Deoxyribonucleic Acid), that the cell of human life (which will reproduce itself) is composed of over 400 parts. Each is positioned in the chain in highly specific order.

What is the probability that all these tiny parts could get together in this highly specific order and do so at random, unaided by a highly intelligent power that could plan and execute the plan?

The answer is found by the same formula we used on the experiment with ten ping pong balls. In this case the formula would be approximately $(1/400)^{244}$ (one over 400 raised to the 244th power). That's 1/400 with 240 zeros following.

Now imagine that one of those balls is painted red and thoroughly shuffled into the mass and thus intermingled with all the others. Call *them* white. What are the chances of getting, while blindfolded, that one red ball out of that white mass on the first try? As already stated, the probability against it is $1/400^{240}$. The difficulty is so great that the human mind cannot grasp the enormous odds against the change of it happening.

Those are the odds against reproducible life coming into existence unaided by an intelligent source of power strong enough and intelligent enough to accomplish the task.

Therefore the basis on which evolution is built is a million miles off target. It is hard to imagine a more shaky foundation. Neither evolution nor its basic starting point is factual. The whole thing is a hypothesis, a theory, a guess.

It is easier to believe that an explosion in a print shop would produce an unabridged dictionary or that three hundred monkeys locked up with three hundred typewriters would produce the works of Shakespeare in a thousand monkey generations than to believe that random chance plus time plus energy could start from zero and produce a race of men and this world, full of life, that includes millions of species, all of which are highly complex creatures.

Notice that word creature: It implies a Creator. That is the most sensible, easy-to-grasp concept that will explain our universe, our world, and the life on it.

If you ask where God came from, who created Him, you are right back where Hebrews 11:3 puts us. It must be accepted by faith, so the evolutionist and the biblicist must start at the same point. If you demand a beginning for God, then try to find a point where space begins, and another point where it ends, a point beyond which there is no space. When you locate that point, then there might be reason to seek a beginning date and place for God's existence!

There is another problem in evolution that removes it from the realm of an exact science and places it where it belongs—as a most unlikely theory. This problem is, How did a single cell of life produce all the species that have life? The entire testimony of experience is that like begets like. There is not one demonstrable event in the history of man to show anything different where species are concerned. The weight of evidence is against evolution and favors biblical creation, which is explicit about the separateness of species (Genesis 1:21-15).

Man always begets man, animals always beget animals, fish beget fish, as fowls beget fowls, and insect beget their own kind, just as Genesis chapter 1 tells us. Each species reproduces itself after its own kind. Of course, there are many possible variations *within* a species, as is explained by Mendel's law of heredity.

There is a law of God that controls all of what we call heredity. An Austrian monk named Mendel did a wonderful work in discovering the laws of heredity, called Mendel's Law of Heredity. The work he had done was buried in the monastery with the flowers he had observed. Had that work been known to Charles Darwin the whole course of the idea and theory of evolution would have been altogether different. But Darwin did not know Mendel's Law of Heredity, and it only came to light as a rediscovery after the furious war over Charles Darwin.

Mendel's Law of Heredity is one of the great laws of God that we have discovered. It is this: the offspring inherit and produce and exhibit the characteristics of the parents according to dominant and recessive characteristics. For example, brown is dominant over blue. If there was a father who was pure brown-eyed and a mother who was pure blue-eyed, all of their children in the first generation would be brown-eyed, following generations differing according to a set pattern.

Mendel's Law of Heredity does two things: It makes possible the breeding of great varieties in a species. For example, one can breed speed into horses. One can have all kinds of flowers by breeding different kinds. One can have all kinds of dogs by breeding different strains of dogs. In the sperm of the male is all the ancestry of the male, and in the ovum of the female is all the ancestry of the female. So when they are brought together there are infinite possibilities of varieties. If you wanted to breed speed in a horse, you pick those varieties and breed them up. If you want to breed the heavy wool on the back of a sheep you take those strains and breed them up. If you want to add more grains on an ear of corn you have infinite opportunity by Mendel's Law to breed up these strains.

There is another fact, according to Mendel's Law, and it is this: Whatever is done to change that variety has to be done to those genes and chromosomes. It can never be done by inherited characteristics. For an offspring to change the parent has to change. The parent is the only one who can give life to an ovum or a sperm.

An embryo can never produce another embryo. It produces another parent. An egg can never produce another egg. It produces a parent which in turn produces another egg. Acquired characteristics are never inherited. You can take a dog and cut off his tail, but when that puppy has puppies they will have tails. And you can cut those tails off, and cut those tails off for a hundred thousand generations, and the puppies that are born will still have tails. You cannot take off or add to by an acquired characteristic. It has to be done in the gene. It has to be done in the chromosome. It has to be done in the nucleus of the ovum or of the sperm.

The only thing that can give life to an ovum or a sperm is a mature parent. So we have an endless cycle that is locked-in by almighty God. God said each after its kind. And the earth gave birth to all of these different kinds of animals and beasts and cattle and creeping things, each after his kind, according to the law of almighty God. Each gives birth to progeny after its kind. (From Criswell, *Did Man Just Happen?* page 44 ff. Zondervan, 1970 edition.)

God's decree that each species is locked into its own kind has never failed. Its boundaries have never been breached. We have thousands of years of evidence to prove this. No scientist, with all his knowledge and skill, can crossbreed between species and develop a new species that will reproduce itself. He can get mutuations, but the species is still the same. A horse can beget a mule when bred to a jackass, but the mule is still in the horse famiy.

Since no evidence can be produced to demonstrate transmutation from one species to another, evolutionistic arguments that it has happened are pure theory—completely hypothetical concepts.

More than a few evolutionists have admitted that the "facts" in evolution are not strong enough to convince them of its validity. What keeps them evolutionists is the "unacceptability of the only alternative." That "unacceptable" alternative is creation. Sir Arthur Keith is one who thought this way. So is Professor D.M.S. Watson of the University of London.

Why is it that the evolutionist will not admit that thing that he sees with his own eyes? Even the great evolutionist

LeComte du Nouy, well-known French scientist, in his book *Human Destiny,* which was hailed as a brilliant contribution to the theory of evolution, admitted: "Each group, order, or family seems to be born suddenly and we hardly ever find the forms which link them to the preceding strain. When we discover them they are *already* completely differentiated. Not only do we find practically no transitional forms, but *in general it is impossible to authentically connect a new group with an ancient one.*" He admits that the reptiles appear suddenly, that they cannot be linked with any of their terrestrial ancestors, and he makes the same admission regarding mammals. About birds he says, "They have all the unsatisfactory characteristics of absolute creation."

Why does LeComte du Nouy refer to absolute creation as being "unsatisfactory"? The answer is this: The evolutionist looks upon special creation as it is recorded by the hand of God in the Book of Genesis as a thing not to be seen and a thing not to be heard and a thing not to be spoken of. He is prejudiced against the creative act of God and he looks upon it as an evil not to be admitted. (From Criswell, *Did Man Just Happen?*)

For example, Sir Arthur Keith said: "Evolution is unproved and unprovable. We believe it because the only alternative is special creation, and that is unthinkable." Professor D.M.S. Watson of the University of London said, "Evolution itself is accepted by zoologists, not because it has been observed to occur or can be proved by logically coherent evidence to be true, but because the only alternative, special creation, is clearly incredible."

I am convinced that it is not creation per se that is objectionable to such people. The fact that creation needs a Creator, is what they cannot accept. They are like those described in Romans 1:21-28, who did not think it worthwhile to retain the knowledge of God in their data.

Many people want to believe God and His Bible as well as evolution. These are called theistic evolutionists. But evolution and the Bible are 180 degrees apart on the story of creation. The Bible speaks of days where evolution speaks of millions and millions of years. The Bible speaks of each species as a separate act of creation, but evolution says that it was all an evolutionary process plus adaptation plus survival of the fittest. Theistic evolution cannot be harmonized with the Bible.

In general, evolution is of two kinds: atheistic evolution and theistic evolution. Atheistic evolution would teach that either matter is eternal or that it was generated by inherent powers apart from a supreme intelligence or Creator. Theistic evolution, on the other hand, admits that there was an "Intelligence" which created the substance of the universe and guided it in its evolutionary development. This intelligence may be personal or impersonal. Theistic evolution can be even more dangerous than atheistic evolution because it does admit of a god of some sort. But when it proceeds to attribute to this God an evolutionary development whereby everything evolved from an original mass, a nebulous or primordial cell, and to that man came up through the lower animals until he evolved in the image of God, then theistic evolution is little better than atheistic evolution.

The Bible story of creation is so clear it admits of no evolution from a lower form to a higher. It says man was created (not evolved) by a separate act of God, and so stands above and apart from all the rest of creation. The Bible record of creation has stood the test of time, while the countless speculations, theories, and guesses of men are strewn, discarded and disproven, along the path of history. We have no quarrel with science—true science; we have no quarrel with evolution if by it we mean the improvement and development of plants and animals within the confines of Bible revelation. But much so-called science is not scientific, and wherever science and Bible conflict, it is either because we have misinterpreted the Bible, or science was wrong and is still in error. There can be no conflict between true science and the correct interpretation of Scripture. God is the Author of true science, for science is the study of natural phenomena and the relations between them. Science deals with matter, the laws which govern it, and the phenomena it manifests; and since God is the Creator of matter and the Author of its laws and manifestations of its phenomena, God is the

Author of true science. Basically nothing is truly scientific unless founded upon absolute fact. Unless substantiated by fact and proven to be a fact, it is only as Paul calls it science. . . . falsely so called." (From M.R. DeHaan, *Genesis and Evolution.* Zondervan.)

Variation *within a species* is demonstrable. Cattle have been bred from scrawny types to huge, heavy, fatted breeds. Pigs have been developed from skinny, razorback animals to huge, sleek, fat hogs. but they are still pigs. Great skill is required to accomplish and maintain this. These and other animals, so interbred, will revert back to their original state if left alone, uncared for, for several generations. They will not continue the selective breeding on their own. That process requires a higher degree of skill and intelligence than the animal possesses. Men must study, experiment, take great risks of failure, and spend money, time, and energy to develop these skills and acquire the body of knowledge that make such selective breeding possible.

When one syncretizes evolution with the Bible account of creation, he is trying to resolve a conflict between two opposing forces, between a thesis and an anti-thesis. By forming a new entity, or force, he then has a synthesis which is neither pure evolution nor pure Bible. He has both added to and taken from the Bible.

God warns that His Word is to be kept pure:

Ye shall not add unto the word which I command you, neither shall ye diminish ought from it, that ye may keep the commandments of the Lord your God which I command you (Deuteronomy 4:2).

What thing soever I command you, observe to do it: thou shalt not add thereto, nor diminish from it (Deuteronomy 12:32).

Violation of these two commands is involved in syncretizing evolution and the Bible.

This chapter is written to describe one of the roots through which psychology has grown (and the soil from which it has drawn much material). Animalistic evolution is part and parcel of all nonbiblical psychology. The Skinnerian behaviorists openly use the belief that man is an animal as a fundamental principle. Darwinism influenced Freud's psychoanalysis and psychotherapy. Neither the humanists nor the transpersonal psychologists deny or renounce it, although they do not make an issue of it, as do the behaviorists. When questioned, they admit their evolutionistic beliefs.

The question I always ask is, "How can any Bible believer be true to the Scriptures and accept *any* dogma that includes things hostile to the God of the Bible?"

16

The Sufficiency of the Scriptures

Psychology claims to have answers to man's problems. I'm not aware of any claim that it has *all* the answers, but it does have some. However, even some of the answers psychology does have are wrong. For example, psychology is wrong when it uses answers to animal behavior as a model for solutions to all human behavior. There are too many variables in man: his power of choice, ability to appreciate, to evaluate, to love, to be saintly or devilish (to name a few). No animals shed accurate light on there factors.

The Bible also claims to have answers to man's problems. But unlike psychology, the Bible does claim to have *all* the answers to *all* of man's real problems. It also insists that none of the answers are wrong.

> Simon Peter, a servant and apostle of Jesus Christ, to those who through the righteousness of our God and Savior Jesus Christ have received a faith as precious as ours:
>
> Grace and peace be yours in abundance through the knowledge of God and of Jesus our Lord.
>
> His divine power has given us everything we need for life and godliness through our knowledge of him who called us by his own glory and goodness.

> Through these he has given us his very great and precious promises, so that through them you may participate in the divine nature and escape the corruption in the world caused by evil desires (2 Peter 1:1-4 NIV).

Note that after Peter greets those to whom his letter was written (verses 1,2) he tells them that God has given them "everything needed for life." He goes on to explain that these necessary things are in those "very great and precious promises" of the Scriptures.

Another witness to this fact is found in Paul's Second Letter to Timothy.

> All Scripture is inspired by God and profitable for teaching, for reproof, for correction, for training in righteousness; that the man of God may be adequate, equipped for every good work (2 Timothy 3:16,17 NASB).

What Paul has said here is that the "tools of a man of God" are the Scriptures, and that they equip him and make him adequate for *every good work*.

This "good work" which the man of God is to do involves helping people be all that God wants them to be. This includes helping them have the "abundant life" Jesus spoke about in John 10:10:

> I have come that they might have life, and that they might have it more abundantly.

The abundant life of which Jesus spoke includes a way of living that is characterized by the fruit of the spirit:

> . . . the fruit of the spirit is love, joy, peace, long-suffering, gentleness, goodness, faith, meekness, temperance (or self-control) (Galatians 5:22,23).

Paul also says that the life which the "man of God" adequaty teaches is:

1. A life in which man is victorious, "more than a conqueror":
   Nay, in all these things we are more than conquerors through him that loved us (Romans 8:37).

2. A life in which man is always triumphant.
   Now thanks be unto God, which always causeth us to triumph in Christ, and maketh manifest the savor of his knowledge by us in every place (2 Corinthians 2:14).

3. A life in which a man can adequately cope with whatever state he finds himself involved:
   For no temptation—no trail regarded as enticing to sin [no matter how it comes or where it leads]—has overtaken you and laid hold on you that is not common to man—that is, no temptation or trial has come to you that is beyond human resistance and that is not adjusted and adapted and belonging to human experience, and such as man can bear. But God is faithful [to His Word and to His compassionate nature], and He [can be trusted] not to let you be tempted and tried and assayed beyond your ability and strength of resistance and power to endure, but with the temptation He will [always] also provide the way out—the means of escape to a landing place—that you may be capable and strong and powerful patiently to bear up under it. (1 Corinthians 10:13 Amplified Bible).

4. A life of contentment:
   Not that I speak in respect of want: for I have learned, in whatsoever state I am, therewith to be content (Philippians 4:11).

   But godliness with contentment is great gain. And having food and raiment, let us be therewith content (1 Timothy 6:6,8).

   Let your conversation be without covetousness, and be content with such things as ye have, for he hath said, I will never leave thee nor forsake thee (Hebrews 13:5).

There are many other characteristics of a Bible-centered life, some of which will be mentioned later. The curious can easily discover enough of such biblical traits to know that people who fit these categories are not neurotics, psychotics, paranoids, schizophrenics, or depressives. They are of sound mind (2 Timothy 1:7):

For God hath not given us the spirit of fear, but of power, and of love, and of a sound mind.

My thesis is that people whose lives are all messed up can get their lives straightened out by proper application of the Scriptures. This proper application can be done by the person who is troubled, whether or not he has access to the help of a man of God. Of course, the ideal would be to have that assistance.

I realize that one does not "prove" his case with examples of successes. But having seen the principles of the Bible actually turn people who had been diagnosed as manic-depressives into calm, vibrant, happy persons, it is easy for me to believe that the Scriptures are all-sufficient to meet serious personal problems.

In my own career as a counselor, I've seen drug addicts set free, schizophrenics become normal, the fearful made bold, the anxious and worried become calm. I've seen serious marital dysfunctions turn into happy marriages, and parent-child warfare turned into peaceful family relationships. I've seen many instances where interpersonal strife was calmed and friendship began to flourish even though enmity had previously abounded. The only guidance used in these cases was that of the Scriptures.

Aside from my personal faith in God's Holy Scriptures, I've seen enough evidence in the hard reality of hundreds of counseling cases to assure me that Paul was correct when he wrote to the Church at Corinth the following words:

> There hath no temptation taken you but such is as common to man, but God is faithful, who will not suffer you to be tempted above that ye are able, but will with the temptation also make a way to escape, that ye may be able to bear it. (1 Corinthians 10:13).

The Greek word *pirasmos*, here translated "temptation," is elsewhere translated as a trial, test, or ordeal. Therefore the word is not limited to an inducement to do something wrong. It can mean any severe ordeal that human beings are subjected to. It is used this way in 1 Peter 4:12:

Beloved, think it not strange concerning the fiery trial which is to try you, as though some strange thing happened unto you.

So Paul's message to the Corinthians could be paraphrased, "There has no test, no ordeal, no trial overtaken you but such as other people experience. In any case God is faithful and will make it possible for you to escape out of them even though you may have to bear them for a while."

To restate it as simply as possible, the Scriptures have an answer for every mental or emotional problem. They are all-sufficient for solving all man's psychological or psychiatric difficulties.

Somone may say, "I know Christians who are not of sound mind but are neurotic (or any of those so-called mental problems mentioned above). How come, if the Bible is so adequate?"

These people are not following the biblical pattern for living, either because of ignorance of what is required or else because they have no well-informed man of God to guide them.

It is unthinkable to believe that God would create a human being and not give him full information on how to live a good, abundant life. To believe that is irreverence at its worst. That sort of neglect on God's part would be like a healthy, wealthy woman bringing a child into the world and then putting it on a ghetto doorstep, leaving it to the mercy of a poverty-stricken society.

This child-abandonment illustration does not tell us anything about ghetto people. Some of the most saintly, godly people on earth are there. Neither does it tell us anything about the child's eventual welfare. He might turn out to be a hero of the faith. Similar things have happened in the past. But this illustration does tell us alot about a woman who would do such a thing, or about God if He left His creation to shift for itself without guidance.

If God had left His created man without directives on how

he should live, Adam would have been blameless and God would appear to have been at fault.

But God did tell Adam all he needed to know in order to live a healthy, prosperous, abundant life. He said, in effect, "Adam, don't ever try to learn the difference between good and evil by experimentation. I want you to take my word for that."

Then He set up one standard as the only test by which Adam's compliance would be judged.

Adam failed even that minimum standard. All the problems that followed this disobedience were Adam's fault. His sin of disobedience was the cause of all his trouble. But God promised Adam a remedy.

Later Cain, Adam's son, became involved in evil behavior:

> Not as Cain, who was of that wicked one, and slew his brother. And wherefore slew he him? Because his own works were evil, and his brother's righteous (1 John 3:12).

Cain was caught up in the backwash from his father's sin, but he himself had become a transgressor by his own evil deeds. Before his evil deeds erupted into murder, God had spoken to him about his problem:

> In the course of time Cain brought some of the fruits of the soil as an offering to the Lord. But Abel brought fat portions from some of the firstborn of his flock. The Lord looked with favor on Abel and his offering, but on Cain and his offering he did not look with favor. So Cain was very angry, and his face was downcast.
>
> Then the Lord said to Cain, "Why are you angry? Why is your face downcast? If you do what is right, will you not be accepted? But if you do not do what is right, sin is crouching at your door; it desires to have you, but you must master it." Now Cain said to his brother Abel, "Let's go out to the field." And while they were in the field, Cain attacked his brother Abel and killed him (Genesis 4:3-8 NIV).

God warned and instructed Cain. He called attention to his anger, to the fact that his behavior was improper. He also explained his rejection and provided a method to gain acceptance. God pointed out that sin other than Cain's own personal sin was also involved, and told him to master that too.

The Bible record will not give all the instances in which God gave instructions to man. The world is too small to hold such a record. But we know that God did speak to man to help, warn, and guide him.

There is not space available in this book to deal with more than a fraction of the highlights of how God gave adequate data to man to help him with his problems.

At the time God gave the Law through the ministry of Moses, He pointed out that these laws were adequate to meet and solve all His people's problems. Keeping them would even guarantee freedom from disease.

> If thou wilt diligently hearken to the voice of the Lord thy God, and wilt do that which is right in his sight, and wilt give ear to his commandments, and keep all his statutes, I will put none of these diseases upon thee, which I have brought upon the Egyptians, for I am the Lord that healeth thee (Exodus 15:26).

> And the Lord will take away from thee all sickness, and will put none of the evil diseases of Egypt, which thou knowest, upon thee, but will lay them upon all them that hate thee (Deuteronomy 7:15).

Through the ministry of the prophets, the psalmists, and the writers of the books of wisdom, God gave adequate instruction to keep His people out of trouble. He thoroughly explained that rejecting His ways were the cause of their problems.

At the proper time God sent His Son with all-sufficient illustrations, lived out in human form. Then He gave adequately trained apostles who had been given teaching that offered all the instruction man needs in order to live abundantly, victoriously, and triumphantly.

Jesus died, was resurrected, was taken up into heaven, and was given all power in heaven and in earth, which he shared with His people. He assured them He was always available to help them with any problem.

Christ sent the Holy Spirit to dwell in those who obeyed His instructions. He gave further inspired writings to His church. Not one necessary thing did He leave out.

When Peter and Paul wrote the words, "His divine power has given all things that pertain to life" and "All Scripture is inspired by God and is profitable for teaching, for reproof, for correction, for training in righteousness, that the man of God may be adequate, equipped for every good work," they said it all.

Doctor Jay Adams in his books *Competent to Counsel, Christian Counselor's Manual,* and *The Use of the Scriptures in Counseling* deals adequately with the theme that the Scriptures are all-sufficient for helping people handle problems.

I firmly believe that the Bible is so completely all-sufficient that if a society had only that one book and no other, and if it followed its principles with total commitment, that society would solve all its spiritual, emotional, and mental problems, —all interpersonal problems with God and man, including parental and marital difficulties and dysfunctions.

The Scriptures need no additives to strengthen them.

> Ye shall not add unto the word which I command you, neither shall ye diminish ought from it, that ye may keep the commandments of the Lord your God which I command you (Deuteronomy 4:2).

> Add thou not unto his words, lest he reprove thee, and thou be found a liar (Proverbs 30:6).

> What thing soever I command you, observe to do it; thou shalt not add thereto nor diminish from it (Deuteronomy 12:32).

> For I testify unto every man that heareth the words of the prophecy of this book, if any man shall add unto these things, God shall add unto him the plagues that are written in this book; and if any man shall take away from the

words of the book of this prophecy, God shall take away
his part out of the book of life, and out of the holy city and
from the things which are written in this book (Revelation
22:18,19).

I admit seeing things in psychology, in philosophy, and in
science that have helped me understand certain applications
of Scripture, but at no time have they added new truth to the
old. The Bible, unaided by any outside source, contains all
that is necessary to life and godliness.

God did not get caught surprised, and have to raise up a
psychology or a philosophy to meet and correct problems He
had overlooked. He saw it all from the beginning and made
ample provision for every contingency.

Humanity has, in general, messed things up quite badly.
The results are weighing heavily upon our entire social structure. Many attempts are made by the sciences to meet the
problems. But in spite of all their attempts, hospitals are over-
flowing, jails are overcrowded, mental asylums are packed,
morals are lower, homosexuals are more numerous and more
blatant, divorce rates soar, and drug abuse and alcoholism in-
crease. As Doctor Hugh Ridleheuber, a psychiatrist and a personal friend, said to me, "Sometimes as I look at the social
structure in which we live, it seems to me its foundations are
crumbling."

Since the sociologists, the philosophers, the psychiatrists,
and the psychologists have not been able to stem the tide by
their methodologies, should they not pause long enough to
determine if the message of the Bible might not be the
answer? I think they should.

There is no question in my mind that a complete compliance with the full biblical methodology is the only thing
that will stem the tide of evil and bring our culture back to
where God intended His creation to be.

17

Where Are
We Headed?

When man ceases to recognize the existence of absolute truth, he tends to swing like a pendulum from one extreme intellectual position to another. History reveals this. During the Middle Ages there was an overemphasis on humanity's spiritual needs, but man's material and physical necessities were neglected. Without absolute truth as a chart and compass, there was no known harbor at which people on an intellectual journey could build a permanent base of operations. For example, neglecting the physical and material wants of man led to a rebellion against the poverty of the Middle Ages. Thus the pendulum of academic research began to swing the other ways, to an overemphasis of materialism, and the Renaissance was born. But it came at the expense of neglecting man's spiritual needs as the search for knowledge rushed to another extreme.

So it has always been. Many in their search for truth are—

> . . . always learning but never able to acknowledge the truth (2 Timothy 3:7 NIV).

This tendency to swing from one overemphasis to an opposite overemphasis is a direct result of denying the existence of absolute truth. Celestial navigation illustrates the importance of fixed reference points. Being forced to navigate the seas without these reference points can lead to disaster. It is likewise *intellectually* disastrous for man to navigate the oceans of knowledge without fixed, unalterable reference points. Otherwise he never really knows with certainty where he is, or even if he is on the right course.

I am aware of the electronic devices that are used as a substitute for stars used in celestial navigation, which devices make it possible to safely navigate the world's oceans and airways. But there are no electronic devices to bring absolute truth to man in his search for knowledge. Computers store knowledge and make calculations and predictions based on knowledge, but they are only as accurate as the data programmed into them. G-I-G-O is still an accurate computer acronym: "Garbage-in, Garbage-out." Nothing better comes out of the computer than that which is put into it.

Unfortunately, the failure to recognize absolute truth about man and God as it is revealed in the Bible is a characteristic of most psychology. As a result, much of it has been studied without a compass and chart having absolute truth as a fixed reference point. Therefore it has swung pendulum-like from one extreme to another—ever learning but never able to acknowledge the (absolute) truth.

We can easily see these swings from one extreme to another in psychology. From psychoanalysis, which was rooted in a study of man's nonmaterial, subconscious mind, the emphasis swung to behaviorism, which totally rejects belief in a nonmaterial mind and insists that man is only a machine-like material being that is predetermined by his chromosomes and genes or reprogrammed by his environment.

Then against the behaviorist extremes came voices of men who said that man is a free moral agent with ability to overcome his environment, make choices, and determine his own destiny. He was portrayed as basically good, with his inner drives biased toward self-improvement. From beliefs that man is a victim of blind chance and fate, the pendulum of emphasis swung to belief that man is his own destiny-maker. Feelings and experiences are the important stuff in man's existence; this was the banner of research in this study of man.

It is totally opposite from behaviorism. This approach in psychological studies is known as the third force, or, more popularly, humanistic psychology. The latter term is used because of the emphasis given to humanity's alleged basic potential goodness.

Then, because no absolute truth was established, too many questions remained unanswered. This was also nurtured by the rapid rate at which the mass of knowledge was accumulating. Cosgrove estimates that knowledge doubles every seven years. On that basis there is eight times as much data to work on now than was available 21 years ago!

In effect, men with unsatisfied appetites to know the truth were saying that nothing in any of the psychological studies had answered all the questions. In fact, there remained more unanswered questions than ever. Studying man empirically, as only a material object, didn't deal with all available data. Neither did psychoanalytic probing provide all the answers. Humanism championed man's fundamental goodness but could not explain why few people, if any, reached the alleged potential. Neither could humanism explain man's abundant evil, crime, wars, inhumanity to fellowman, racialism, greed, and other abuses of himself and his contemporaries.

So, if looking *at* man or *into* man fails to answer all the questions about man, why not look *beyond* man? Thus "Transpersonal Psychology" came into the academic scene. In its earliest stages it was sort of a hybrid psychology, a newstand, magazine-rack variety, but by the time the 1960s arrived it had enough academic strength to be called the fourth force in psychology.

"Looking beyond man" meant looking at his altered mental state of conscious awareness. That is, it studies man's states of conscious awareness while he is under the influence of hallucinogenic drugs, or meditations and dreams, or in euphoric states of mind, or in other similar states of awareness.

But neither does transpersonal psychology have absolute truth for checkpoints. Therefore, its scholars are rapidly getting into foggy mysticism. This time the pendulum has swung beyond any position taken previously. It is a new ball game, at least for Western culture.

However, many critical questions still remain unanswerable by all four psychological forces. Those questions will not go away, either! They will actually grow more numerous as time continues, for the rate of additional knowledge keeps accelerating.

Nevertheless, there is a bright star of hope on the horizon. Although psychology scholars seem unable to arrive at absolute truth, there is a lot of intellectual honesty coming to the surface.

Recently seven leaders in the fields of psychology and counseling met to study points where they had conflicting ideologies, or misunderstandings about psychological positions that touched Bible doctrines. They also had some personal as well as academic differences.

Dr. John F. Bettler, director of the Christian Counseling and Educational Foundation, in Laverock, Pennsylvania, chaired this conference.

A general letter from Dr. Bettler, reporting on this meeting, arrived on my desk as I was working on this chapter. I immediately phoned him, congratulated him, and asked for permission to quote his letter. Here it is.

Dear Counseling Friends:

I sat at the table suffering from the strange blending of eager anticipation and not-so-subtle foreboding. Before me sat six of the best-known Christian psychologists and counselors in the country, each a respected author and educator and each a strong personality with strongly held convictions.

Months of prayer, hard-nosed planning and budgeting had prepared the way for this meeting. I was relieved that all of that was behind me. "But," I said to myself, "What happens now? Perhaps this wasn't such a good idea after all. What if a meeting designed to bring these men together actually drove the wedge of division deeper?"

I thought, "Let's pray." And we did. One by one the men prayed for the love of Christ, for graciousness and gentleness and for the honor of God. My fears began to melt away.

Henry Brandt started off with his paper, "What is Biblical Counseling?" His unaffected and straightforward plea to honor the Bible in counseling was so winsome and warmly presented that we all began to relax and realize that the God of the Scriptures is the sure and solid foundation on which to work.

Larry Crabb followed, introducing more of the psychological data with which we must grapple, but with the same commitment to the authority of Scripture.

Then the others: John Carter, Gary Collins, Jay Adams and Bruce Narramore. Each position was clearly outlined —the differences becoming more apparent—but all was done in a spirit of Christian compassion.

The day ended. No catastrophies. Thank you, Lord.

But what about the next day? That was the time for dialogue and debate of substantive issues.

"Let's start off safe," I thought. So, I introduced the problem of common grace and general revelation—an important issue in the integration of theology and psychology.

The men politely dealt with it. But their hearts weren't in it. They wanted to get to other issues. Soon they hurled questions like: "What did you mean when . . ." "How would you . . ." "Can you really support that argument?" They strained to understand one another.

At times the debate was heated. Some differences between them are marked and, because of the considerable investment the men have made, will not be easily surrendered. But, overall, the atmosphere was cordial and helpful. Here was a group of men eager to know one another and to strengthen the cause of Christian counseling.

That is the kind of dialogue which took place. There is so much more I could tell you about these exciting two days, but now is not the time. The complete papers and dialogue will be published, we hope, by this Fall.

But, now please rejoice with us for these meetings. And pray that the results will continue—that unity will be cemented where possible, that division will be handled in compassion, that the Bible will not be compromised and that God will be honored in the development of true Christian counseling.

Sincerely,

John F. Bettler
Director

These men have absolutes in their charts as they navigate through the vast oceans of data about man now available. They are striving to never compromise the teaching of God's Word.

In spite of the confusion in psychology, it is heartening to realize that some of the best-known Christian psychologists, who are educators and authors, are using God's absolute truth as chart and compass. May God grant that thousands of other leaders will swell the ranks of those who base their convictions on the changeless Word of God.